DIVORCE STEP BY STEP

DIVORCE
STEP BY STEP

———

A Practical Guide to Navigating the Challenges Ahead

René Vercoe

ROCKRIDGE
PRESS

For general information on our other products and services or to obtain technical support, please contact our Customer Care Department within the United States at (866) 744-2665, or outside the United States at (510) 253-0500.

Rockridge Press publishes its books in a variety of electronic and print formats. Some content that appears in print may not be available in electronic books, and vice versa.

"Letter to the Editor" used courtesy of *The Daily Nebraskan*.

Interior and Cover Designer: Rachel Haeseker
Art Producer: Samantha Ulban
Editor: Mo Mozuch
Production Editor: Matthew Burnett

Cover Art © M. by mprintly/Creative Market.

ISBN: Print 978-1-64739-279-6 | eBook 978-1-64739-280-2

R0

This book is dedicated to my children, Jessica, Logan, and Claire . . . and, yes, even to my ex, Mike.

CONTENTS

INTRODUCTION

Welcome to the club you never wanted to be a part of—**the Divorcée Club**. I certainly never thought I'd be a part of it, but divorce happens to half the people who get married. It happened to me, and now it's happening to you. Wrapping your brain around it is tough, but moving through the legal process is even tougher. Divorce tops the list of life's most stressful moments, right up there with changing careers, making a long-distance move, and the death of a loved one. In some ways it is like a death: a death of dreams and the death of a relationship.

It is also a time of many questions. What is happening to your life? What will it look like when you're no longer married? Where will you live? How will you pay for it? What happens to the kids? Will you have to go to work? Will you sell the house? Do you need an attorney?

This book is meant to help you find answers to these questions. It is my hope that you'll soon understand your options and lay a road map for moving through this process so that you **not only survive but thrive** in the future. You will do well to take control where you can and accept where you can't.

The road to becoming a Certified Divorce Coach was an unexpected one, yet I can now say it is one of the most fulfilling journeys of my life. After 27 years of marriage and three children, I found myself going through a painful and messy divorce. Completely overwhelmed, paralyzed with fear, angry at my spouse, and terrified of what lay ahead, I unknowingly found myself on the way to a career that I did not even know existed. Figuring out where to begin in my divorce seemed too much to contemplate. Because I had no road map, I was always in a defensive position and reacting to whatever came at me from attorneys, courts, children, banks, and my own emotionally stressed mind. It caused a lot more pain on all sides than was necessary and cost tens of thousands of dollars more than it ever should have. In the end, the only winners were the attorneys.

With this book, I hope to help you avoid some of the mistakes I made by giving you insight on what lies ahead. It is a step-by-step guide to help you get organized and stay focused at a difficult time. The goal is to maintain control where you can, make educated decisions, and take your power back so you can move forward with confidence.

As a Certified Divorce Coach, I can promise you no two divorces are the same. However, the one constant I see in every divorce is the overwhelming chaos and upheaval that can leave you paralyzed. Fear of the unknown is terrifying, but you can help yourself through this time by educating yourself about the process. Knowing what to expect is the best way to overcome these feelings, and since you are reading this book, you are already on the path to knowledge. Knowing what to expect is going to be your greatest asset in **turning the chaos into confidence**.

How to Use This Book

This book is not a replacement for professional, legal, or financial advice. It is meant to answer many of the questions you might have and guide you through the process ahead. It will help you formulate the specific questions to ask each professional you work with along the way, should you decide they will be helpful to your situation.

Lawyers, accountants, retirement specialists, therapists, etc., are largely paid by the hour, so knowing the role each professional plays in the process is important. Attorneys are there to help you get through the legal and financial part of divorce fairly and equitably, but they are not there to be your therapist. A financial advisor helps organize your finances; they are not an attorney. A therapist is there to help you with the emotions of your divorce; they are not a financial advisor or an attorney. And a divorce coach is there to steer you in the right direction when you're stuck.

This book will help you understand whether each of the aforementioned professionals is the right one to assist you with the issues and challenges that you are encountering and assist you with knowing what to address with each of them in order to get the maximum help for the dollars invested. Additionally, you will understand the legal process and terminology and hopefully know what to expect as your divorce unfolds. No two divorces are the same; yours will have its own story. Through this book, I hope to give you the tools to **control the outcome of your story** as much as possible.

This book isn't meant to heal your emotional wounds; there are many books out there to help with that. Rather, it is meant to give you a basic understanding of the divorce process. There are two types of divorce you will find yourself going through: the legal divorce and the emotional divorce. I'm going to walk you through the legal process so you will have a basic understanding of what to expect as you approach your final resolution.

I learned the hard way that there is great reward in keeping your head and your integrity throughout this process. As a result, I would like to help you find a way to survive the process with your dignity intact and keep the respect of those in your life whose opinions you find important. This may be one of the most challenging and difficult periods of your life, but you can come out of it with a new sense of who you are and what you are capable of. Taking the high road not only will help your relationship with your soon-to-be ex-spouse, but it also will solidify your sense of self and your self-dignity. **The process is never easy, but it can be civil**. Now let's get started on this journey.

CHAPTER ONE

I'm Getting Divorced

Despite the uniqueness of every divorce, each proceeds in a step-by-step manner, and one phase will follow the next until completion. Just realizing that you are completing the stages and moving forward may reassure you that there will be a conclusion to the chaos. At times it may feel like there is no end in sight, but there is, and I promise that you will get there.

After years of coaching people through this, there is one thing that always that holds true: Your emotions want to control the process in the beginning, but **it will benefit you greatly to let your intellect and reasoning take charge**. Even when you think you're divorcing a jerk, taking the high road will pay off in the long run. If you make the conscious decision to lead with common sense, even though you may be hurting, you will undoubtedly find that it expedites the resolution of your case. As a result, you will be able to look back on these challenging times with your head held high, knowing that you handled them with grace.

You Are Not Alone

Nancy and Stan were married at 18 and 20 years old, respectively. Both worked menial jobs until they made the decision to venture out together and opened a successful restaurant in their 30s. They had two healthy boys and a house, and the restaurant did well enough that they managed to put away money for retirement and expand the business by opening another restaurant across town. However, having the other restaurant meant that they often found themselves working apart for long hours, and eventually Stan had an affair. When Nancy found out, she was furious and hurt. She wanted to work it out, but after two years of trying, she just didn't feel they could ever get back the trust that had been lost.

They filed for divorce, and with the boys' best interests at heart, they tried the mediation route. They decided it would be best to keep the house and handle the custody through "nesting," where the parents move in and out of the family home each week instead of the kids having to move back and forth between an unfamiliar new home and their "old" home. This would also allow the boys to stay in their schools and would cause the least amount of disruption to their world. After the boys finished school and went to college, Stan and Nancy agreed to sell the house to help fund their educations. They also agreed to split everything else right down the middle, including their ownership interests in the restaurants. In the end, they were able to successfully get their sons through college and amicably co-parent for years.

This is an example of how a successful mediation can help find creative solutions that fit the uniqueness of each situation without giving those decisions over to a judge who isn't familiar with the people involved or the intricacies of the scenario.

The divorce of Henry and Tonya is another success story. Henry spent 30 years with his wife, Tonya, raising a beautiful family of four children who were now all grown and out on their own. They had been married when they were young and in college, both working to keep their heads above water. They lived in a small apartment while Henry finished school. He and Tonya then moved to a small home where they welcomed their first child. Henry was hired by a small insurance company, and Tonya worked part-time as a secretary. Over time, Henry went on to work for a larger company and built a successful portfolio of clients that supported the growing family quite well over the next several years. They weathered a child's grave illness and death and still hung together, believing it had only made them stronger.

Fast-forward a few decades, however, and they seemed to take different paths. Henry made the decision that he wanted to focus on being physically fit and active, whereas Tonya had settled into a relaxed lifestyle where she preferred to do crafts and stay at home most of the time. This departure from common interests seemed to balloon over the next five years, and they soon found themselves as solely room-mates. They both wondered if they were missing something by not having partners that shared their separate interests and were able to calmly communicate their concerns to each other. Though they still loved each other, they were no longer "in love" with each other. They agreed to look at the possibility of splitting up and what this would mean financially for each of them.

By exploring the benefits of doing a legal separation versus a medi-ated divorce, they were able to figure out that it would behoove them to do a legal separation so that Tonya would still have medical insur-ance and the benefits that had been provided to her through marriage. They divided up their property and decided to live apart. Because nei-ther of them had a remarriage in mind at that time, a legal separation worked for them, and it is still in place five years later.

I urge you to take these stories to heart as you begin your divorce journey. You are not alone in this, and for many people, divorce is the right decision at the right time. Of course, it may not seem that way right now, which is why it's so important to recognize the value of having an emotional support system.

Establishing Your Support System

Keeping your emotions in check during this time will pay off in the way you feel about yourself going forward and possibly keep you from wasting thousands of dollars on legal fees. The best outcome is a fair and equitable division of property and assets and to do what is best for the children in the long run. This is what the courts will do, but there are much better ways to get there that will cause less pain to you, your family, and your bank account. Do you really want to give control over these decisions to a judge who doesn't know a thing about you or your family?

Fifty years ago, Elisabeth Kübler-Ross interviewed thousands of people who were dying, and from that research she wrote a book on coping with death called *On Death and Dying*. Her study determined the five stages of grief a person goes through when they know death is imminent: denial, anger, bargaining, depression, and acceptance. These five stages can also apply to divorce in much the same way. Kübler-Ross said that the stages do not necessarily always occur in the same order, and they may overlap to some extent, but each person will travel through these emotional stages at their own pace and eventually accept the truth of their situation.

If you are preparing for a divorce, it is important to know the people you are going to lean on as you go through the process. Who is this for you?

Friends, family, spiritual advisor. I encourage you to find one or two people whom you can trust to be there when you need them for emotional support or just to pick up the kids from school when you have a schedule conflict. You can have more than one person, of course, but you should have at least one person who will be there to step in and assist. When people ask if they can help, don't be ashamed to say *yes*. Call on these people to do research for you, to help with daily tasks, or to let you talk through decisions that you need to make.

Support groups. Groups are sometimes a good resource to help you connect with people going through the same thing you are. You can find these groups online by searching for "divorce support groups" or by checking with your church or community center. Meetup.com usually has some groups listed if you are in an area that has that resource available. It's sometimes nice to have someone to talk to who isn't a part of your circle of friends and family.

Certified Divorce Coach. Perhaps you need some nonlegal professional support to provide practical assistance in navigating your divorce. Your coach will help you understand your emotions and help you keep them in check while also coaching you through the big decisions and explaining the process as it unfolds. They can allow you to vent and then help you clarify your priorities and support you in setting and reaching your ultimate goals.

Therapist. You may find that you could use some help with supporting your mental health. This is vital, as it may be affecting your overall well-being. A therapist will help you find solutions to stubborn personal or family issues and identify if further treatment is necessary.

Physician. Should you be feeling run-down or anxious, having trouble sleeping, or just not yourself, a visit to your physician may be in order. They can be an important part of your support team by offering medical solutions or resource recommendations since they have seen the physical reactions to divorce many times before. If you are concerned that getting help with your emotional health will reflect poorly should you end up in court, be reassured: a judge looks kindly on someone who acknowledges needing help and seeks it out.

Before You File

Whether you are the one who wants the divorce, it's mutual, or you have been completely blindsided by it, there are some simple steps you need to take to protect yourself going forward. You may be thinking that your divorce will go smoothly with little acrimony and you don't need to take these steps, but I assure you, when the finances get involved, things can heat up quickly, and you will want to be sure you are protected. Here is a list that will help:

Put the children first. There's no way to keep them from being affected, but minimizing the pain should be one of your first priorities. Their lives will be significantly impacted no matter what, so think ahead to try to plan a way to provide as much normalcy and stability as possible during this time and after.

Talk to an attorney. Even if you don't hire one to represent you going forward, you need to consult one to find out what your local laws and legal rights are in terms of your living and financial situations and custody of your children. You wouldn't want to jeopardize your home ownership or other assets, so spending the money to have an initial consult with a family law attorney is well worth it. Ask friends for a referral or look on Avvo.com.

Open your own bank account. If you don't already have a checking and savings account that is only in your name, open one as soon as you can so you can keep your money separate from your spouse's money. You will need money for legal fees if your spouse has control of shared assets. Use a different bank from the one that you use for your family accounts, change any direct deposits to this new account, and keep your living expenses in this account.

Get a copy of your credit report. A credit report will tell you where all the family's money is and what charges are being made to the credit cards. If your spouse is responsible for making mortgage payments, credit card payments, etc., you need to be able to track whether they are continuing to make these payments.

Get a credit card in your own name. You will want to start establishing your own credit separate from your spouse, and it may be difficult to get a card once you are divorced if you are not yet employed. Additionally, be sure to call the credit card company and let them know the situation if you have a joint credit card. It would be best to close that account, but often they won't let you without the other party's approval, and if there is a balance on the card, it will need to be dealt with in the financial settlement part of the process. Sometimes a credit card company will close your account just because publicly filing for divorce suddenly makes you a high-risk customer!

Close all joint accounts. If you can't get your spouse to cooperate in closing joint accounts, alert the credit card company of your new relationship status (separated) so that the account is flagged in the event your spouse starts making major purchases.

Get a post office box. Change your mailing address to a post office box and forward your mail to it. You will be getting legal papers, your own bank and credit card statements, and other correspondence that needs to be kept private.

Change your will and your living will. Your spouse is probably the executor of your will and possibly the sole beneficiary. Many states won't allow you to change this until your divorce is final, but you will want to be aware of it. Additionally, if you have an advanced directive for your health care, you probably don't want them making your life-and-death decisions anymore. That is something you can change right away.

Get your financial records in order. You will want to keep these at a friend's or relative's home (or in a safe-deposit box) where only you will have access to them. You will need a copy of your joint tax returns, proof of your income and spouse's income, a copy of your mortgage, bank statements, credit card statements, and evidence of any major purchases. There is a more comprehensive checklist later in this chapter (see page 17).

Types of Divorce

Every state has different laws regarding divorce, so keep that in mind. You will want to go to your state's family law section of their website to learn more about what the specifics are in your state. Whether your state has a fault or no-fault statute will make a difference depending on your own situation. Additionally, your divorce can be contested or uncontested. This doesn't mean whether you want it or not, it means whether you can come to an agreement on division of assets and property, child and marital support, and custody without fighting it out in court. For specific information on filing for divorce in your state, go to divorcenet .com/topics/filing-for-divorce. This site lists the specifics for each state.

The first five of the following options relate to uncontested divorce, and the last pertains to a court trial or contested divorce:

- **Summary divorce.** Short-term marriages that don't have any children, shared debts, assets, or income. Relatively simple paperwork that doesn't require an attorney, often only one filing fee.
- **Default divorce.** When one party doesn't respond to a divorce petition. Again, basic paperwork to resolve that usually doesn't require an attorney but might in some cases.
- **Mediated divorce.** A professionally trained mediator helps both parties develop a settlement agreement on their own without involving the courts. Often far less expensive than a contested divorce and typically ends more amicably.
- **Collaborative divorce.** Both parties hire an attorney with the goal of settling out of court through negotiations and four-way meetings. Longer process than mediation but also tends to be cheaper and less divisive than contested divorce.
- **Arbitrated divorce.** A private judge hired by both spouses hears the case outside a courtroom. This is faster and possibly

less expensive than a courtroom trial with more privacy, though this is not allowed in all states.

- **Contested divorce.** Both spouses hire lawyers and go to trial. This is the most expensive and stressful path a divorce can take. It seriously jeopardizes the chances of a civil relationship between spouses and is especially hard on children.

The Petition Process

If you are the one filing, there are steps you can take prior to filing that will make things easier for you once the process is started. When you file the petition, the court will automatically put an order in place that keeps both of you from taking any of your jointly owned property. You will need to leave any joint savings, checking, and investment accounts as they are unless you and your spouse agree to use them together. The court could also issue temporary support orders, should there be a significant disparity of income between the two of you, so that no one is left with nothing to live on. You and your spouse both share a legal responsibility, prior to filing and after filing, to not do anything that would harm your jointly owned interests, and you certainly can't do anything that would harm your spouse's personal property. I encourage you to seek out examples of divorce petitions online. Your associated state website will also have the forms accessible to you.

Basic Information

A divorce petition, or Petition for the Dissolution of Marriage or Registered Partnership, is simply a document to initiate the legal process. It is signed by the person filing for divorce and then it is filed with the court. It states in very broad terms what the petitioner is asking the court to order. The document is not used to ask for relief (*resolution*), but rather it is the document necessary to begin the legal action associated with the divorce.

If you don't yet have an attorney or hope to navigate your divorce without an attorney, there are a few terms you will need to know.

Clerk of court. You'll file your divorce papers with the court clerk at the county courthouse. The court clerk is the person who works in what is the court system's front office. They handle almost every piece of paperwork that comes into or leaves the court. They are not lawyers and are not allowed to give legal advice; however, they will help you find the papers you need and tell you how to fill them out and what to do next.

Forms. Most states have fill-in-the-blanks legal forms for divorce cases. Usually you can get these at your local courthouse or from the state's website. Here are some of the forms you'll probably need:

- The **petition** or **complaint** starts the divorce process.

- A **summons** that will need to be served to your spouse, along with the petition (this is often done by an agent of the court, such as a sheriff's deputy or process server). It tells your spouse that you are suing for divorce and orders both of you not to dispose of marital assets or make changes on insurance or other documents, not to take your children out of state without the other's permission, and not to do anything else to disturb the status quo.

- A **cover sheet** that you must submit in some places along with your forms to provide information such as what county you live in, how many children you have, and how long you have been married.

- **Financial information sheets** that you give either to the court or to your spouse early in the process (discussed more later).

- **Responsive forms** used by your spouse to file a response to your petition for divorce (possibly required to be delivered with the petition and summons).

- A **proof of service** form that shows the date that your spouse was served the divorce paperwork and describes how it was delivered.

Forms, and specifically petitions, can vary greatly from court to court and can be from one to forty pages, so you will want to obtain a form from your court clerk or county website to see what information you will need. Some states require different forms for marriages with or without children, for contested or uncontested divorce, and for fault or no-fault divorces. Most, though, will require:

- The date and place you were married

- The date of your separation

- Whether you have children and, if so, their names, ages, and birth dates

- Your reason for seeking a divorce (e.g., irreconcilable differences, adultery, etc.)

Some forms let you say what you are seeking in the divorce as far as division of property, child custody and support, and whether you want to change your name. I once had a client who didn't like her maiden name either, so after her divorce she changed her last name to that of her favorite actor!

Residency. One of the first new vocabulary words you will be asked to become familiar with is *residency requirement*. You are normally required to file for divorce in the county in which you live, not in which you got married. Your county may also have a time that you are required to have lived there prior to filing (usually six months to a year), so if you have just moved, you may need to file in your old county. Your county website or attorney will be able to help you with this. If you or your spouse is in the military, residency requirements don't apply, and you can usually file where the military spouse is stationed.

Grounds for divorce. Grounds are the legal reason that you want the marriage to end. Acceptable grounds differ from state to state and may include some or of all the following:

- **Cruel and inhuman treatment.** Physical, psychological, verbal, and/or sexual abuse that makes your continued living together unsafe for you and/or your children.

- **Adultery.** Any sexual act with a person other than the spouse during the period of the marriage.

- **Prison term.** If one of the spouses has been incarcerated for a crime (with length of incarceration time determined by the state).

- **Abandonment.** When one has left the other for a continuous period defined by the state (usually a year or more) without cause or without the other spouse's consent.

- **Constructive abandonment.** When one spouse refuses sex with the other for a period of one year or more without the other spouse's consent.

- **Separation.** Living apart for a period in anticipation of a permanent split through a legal agreement or otherwise depending on state law.

- **Irreconcilable differences.** Also known as *irretrievable breakdown* in the relationship, meaning the two spouses can no longer tolerate living together and the relationship cannot be repaired. States that accept this as grounds for divorce usually set a minimum time the situation has been unbearable, such as six months to a year.

- **No-fault divorce.** Neither party must prove that the other has done anything wrong. In a no-fault divorce, which most states permit, a spouse cannot threaten to contest the proceeding, so there is no ugly courtroom battle even if the fight over property division may be contentious.

Should you be the filing party, you will want to decide the grounds that will be **legally acceptable** in your state **and advantageous** to your side. Unless you live in a no-fault state, you will need to prove these grounds by showing legal fact. Proof most often comes into play when trying to prove adultery. Gathering evidence can be tricky even with all the technology available today, such as email, phone logs, phone bills, and bank and credit card statements that track expenditures. Before you download these or copy records that are in your spouse's name, consult your attorney to be sure you aren't breaking any laws. Using your spouse's password on a computer without their permission can be considered felony computer misuse in some cases.

Choose the process. Now you are ready to determine whether your divorce will be *contested* or *uncontested*.

Uncontested divorce (usually done through mediation or collaboration of your attorneys) means you and your spouse worked out how to end the marriage, how to divide the assets and property, and child custody and support. If you can work out all these issues prior to filing, congratulations! You have just saved yourself thousands of dollars in legal fees and saved a lot of time in the process, too.

Contested divorce, on the other hand, is where you and your spouse have not agreed on one or more of these issues. You may disagree on the grounds, or perhaps one doesn't want a divorce; more often, you disagree on property division or custody. In this case, you end up with dueling attorneys who try to pound out a settlement, and if they can't, it goes to court and a judge decides for you. This can run from $20,000 to over $100,000. So, if you are feeling vengeful and just want to inflict pain, think long and hard about it. *The attorneys are usually the only winners in a contested divorce.*

Temporary Support

If you make the decision to separate but one of you doesn't work or does not have adequate income, it could easily result in that party ending up in dire financial straits. If your spouse has been supporting the family, you're entitled to continued support. If you've been working but your spouse has not, your spouse will be entitled to continued support from you. Should your spouse not voluntarily pay you marital and/or child support, or vice versa, the court can be petitioned and will subsequently order the supporting party to make support payments during the divorce proceeding. This is called temporary support or **pendente lite** ("during litigation") support, and the court will make more permanent support orders later in the process.

If you wish to file for temporary support right away and your spouse is not in agreement, you should talk to an attorney. You may have to come up with the money to see the attorney initially, but there is a chance the court will order your spouse to pay part of your legal fees right away and possibly all of them later. If both of you can come up with an agreement for temporary support without going to court, you could both save on legal fees. However, a word of caution: you are also giving leverage to your spouse, should they abruptly decide not to make a payment. An initial consultation with an attorney will help answer some of the questions regarding how your individual state works to level the financial playing field during the process.

Serving the Papers

After you have filed the initial petition with the court, the next step is to have the papers served to your spouse. Though it sounds simple, they must be delivered in a legally approved manner according to your state's law. You cannot serve the papers yourself. You must have someone else do it and have them sign a document called a "proof of service" stating that they did so. In most cases, you can hire a process server to deliver the documents or ask a friend to do it, or the local sheriff's office will handle it. Your local court clerk will be able to help provide you with your options for this step of the process. If you are considering doing this process without an attorney, let this be a first lesson that half the battle is doing the paperwork correctly, in the eyes of the court.

You can also serve divorce papers by mail and include a form your spouse will sign to acknowledge that the papers were received, but you'll want to have someone else drop it in the mailbox and sign the proof of service form because **you cannot serve the papers yourself.** When serving by mail, should your spouse not return the form, you will need to start over from the beginning. Should your spouse be missing and you are asking for a default divorce, you'll have to ask the court to either allow you to serve your spouse by publication (newspaper or community order) or release you from the obligation to serve your spouse.

Once you have served the papers, you will need to let the court know of the service by filing a form called **proof of service *or* declaration of service** with the court clerk (your new best friend) after having the person who served the papers sign it and enter where, when, and how your spouse was served.

How to Respond to the Petition

If you are the one who is served with papers, you now have the option to file responsive documents with the court or else choose to let the case proceed by default. A **response form** is an answer to the petition and usually looks much like the petition. The response asks the respondent to set out many of the same facts that are asked in the petition. It's meant to determine whether you are both in agreement about such things as how long you've been married, when you separated, and where you and your children live. This form also allows the respondent to disagree with any requests that were made in the petition, like those relating to division of property. If this has all been worked out and it is an uncontested divorce, there shouldn't be any surprises in the response. The court may request other financial documents to be filed along with the response, such as a financial disclosure form, and the court clerk can help you locate this form.

What to Do If You Don't File First

Should I file first? People often wonder if they need to be the first to file for divorce, but this depends on the circumstances. Normally in the eyes of the court, it doesn't matter who files the initial paperwork. That said, your attorney may advise you to file first or wait until your spouse files based on the overall strategy for your case. For example, should there be concern that your spouse will begin transferring assets when they learn about your plans to divorce, your attorney may advise you to move quickly to file the petition so the assets are frozen by the *automatic temporary restraining orders* (ATROs), which are clear in the summons (the petition served to your spouse). These orders keep either party from transferring or otherwise disposing of assets outside the normal course of family living expenses. On the other hand, should you already be separated and have an agreement that is working in your favor, your attorney may suggest you wait for your spouse to file.

In most states, once you are served with the petition, the clock immediately starts. You will typically have 20 to 30 days to respond. If you fail to answer in the allotted time frame, an attorney can usually file a motion and ask the judge for permission to **file an answer out of time**.

If you are at all confused about what the paperwork means, now is the time to consult with an attorney. Even if you choose not to use an attorney as the case proceeds, you should always speak with one initially to make sure you understand your legal rights and responsibilities. They can give you advice on how to represent yourself, explain if there are options to hire an attorney just to file the response, offer advice during the divorce process, or represent you in court. You will want to assess your own situation as to whether you think you will be able to do a do-it-yourself divorce or will need the help of an attorney on the case.

Do not refuse to be served the papers; this will not help your case. Simply accept them, and when your emotions are well under control, go about reading them and filling out the correct forms, which will then need to be filed with the court clerk at the courthouse. Should you need further forms, the clerk will be able to get them for you or help you fill them out. You will need to start getting together your financial papers next, so buckle up!

Financial Checklist

One of the first things you need to do is gather as much financial information about your marriage as you can. This will protect you from a spouse running off with assets as well as provide information for later decisions. Include all your property and debts, even the ones you think belong only to you or only to your spouse. It's especially important to list any debts that you believe are solely your spouse's responsibility so you can make sure your final divorce order makes clear that you're not responsible for them. Additionally, you should include anything that you owned prior to the marriage and think is yours alone. Along with making a written record, it's not a bad idea to make a video recording of your major assets to document the condition at the time you separated and to document how you were living before the divorce because it can sometimes come into play in determining support.

If you decide to use an attorney, they will probably provide you with their own list of documents and information they will need; however, here is a list of the basics you will need to get started:

ASSETS

☐ Checking and savings account information

☐ Stocks, bonds, mutual funds, and money market accounts

☐ Certificates of deposit

- [ ] Real estate (house, condo, or any other property you own, even a time-share)

- [ ] Medical savings account (MSA)

- [ ] Retirement plans, including pensions, 401(k)s, IRAs, SEP IRAs, profit sharing, and any type of deferred compensation plan

- [ ] Cars and any type of vehicles, including boats or recreation vehicles

- [ ] Valuable personal property such as art, jewelry, or collections

- [ ] Furniture

- [ ] Life insurance policies with cash value

- [ ] Season tickets to sporting or cultural events

- [ ] Airline miles and other rewards points

- [ ] Tax refunds you expect

- [ ] Accrued vacation time

DEBTS

- [ ] Mortgage

- [ ] Home equity line of credit

- [ ] Credit cards

- [ ] Vehicle loans

- [ ] Promissory notes

- [ ] Student loans

- [ ] Any other financial obligations

Additionally, you will want to make copies of the documents in the following list. If they are in a safe-deposit box, take a friend or ask a bank employee to witness you opening the box, make a video of the contents, and make a written inventory. Don't take anything from the box unless it belongs to only you. In that case, you'll want to rent a second safe-deposit box and move the contents over to the new box, as it may become necessary that you identify the item(s) and have the court determine that it is in fact your separate property. There is more information on what is considered marital and separate property in chapter 3.

Make copies of the following documents:

- Deeds

- Recent mortgage statements

- Insurance policies

- Retirement plan documents

- Business interests

- Bank brokerage and retirement account statements

- Tax returns for past five years

- Wills and trusts

If your spouse is not cooperating in giving you access to these documents and information, the courts will force them to give you the information after you file. In the meantime, **you can get copies of your tax returns from the IRS** by submitting a simple form (Form 4506), which you can get at irs.gov or by calling 1-800-829-1040.

Don't Get Blindsided

The longer a divorce drags on, the less chance it has of being amicable and the more likely it will get downright ugly. You will want to get as much as you can for your side, but you need to remember this is a negotiation. Assets must be divided. The clock is ticking, and billable hours add up quickly as you work with attorneys or mediators. **Decide now what is an absolute deal-breaker for you and what doesn't matter too much.** Be honest. Keep your emotions in check, and if they are getting out of hand during a settlement meeting, ask to take a break or meet later. Other than your nonnegotiables, try the give-and-take method.

I once saw a couple go to court because she wouldn't give up the outdoor barbecue. She could have bought twenty of them for what she spent on legal fees, and in the end, she actually paid $10,000 for a $500 barbeque. Be smart: No one gets everything they want during a divorce, so stay calm and march on. Don't get caught up in anger or revenge. It has a real cost.

CHAPTER TWO

Do I Need a Lawyer?

As we've discussed, there are multiple types of divorce, and deciding on a strategy for yours will help you determine the type of professionals you will need to help you accomplish your best result. In this chapter we'll delve deeper into *pro se* divorce, mediators, and lawyers. Only 1 in 20 divorces go all the way to trial, so there is a good chance that you will be able to resolve your divorce if you choose the right track from the beginning.

The Right Divorce

Sally and John had been married for 22 years and had three children. John was a pilot, and Sally worked part-time in advertising sales. When she found out that John was having his third extramarital affair in as many years, she knew it was time to move forward with ending the marriage. She anticipated a knock-down, drag-out court battle that would leave them both embattled and broke, but she didn't think he would be fair in the negotiations unless she had an attorney standing up for her. Both wanted what was best for the children and wanted to maintain a good relationship afterward, even though they agreed there was no hope of reconciliation.

Both wanted to reach a fair and mutual agreement, and neither wanted to get shortchanged. They agreed to try mediation, mostly to save money; however, they found it had some real benefits. The mediation sessions were focused and always working toward the end goal of resolving the property division and custody issues but also had a fringe benefit of teaching the two how to communicate in their new relationship. Though this wasn't therapy, and mediators are certainly not counselors, having a third party help them communicate became the first step in building their new relationship going forward.

One of the ways to take some control over the tone of your divorce is through the type of professionals you choose to use during the divorce process. The most common options include:

- **Professional mediator.** You both agree to use a mediator skilled in helping couples come to an equitable agreement regarding the issues surrounding property, spousal support, and child support and custody. This option removes the court from the process until you have an agreement and can file an uncontested divorce petition.

- **Collaborative attorney.** You each select an attorney who works together with you and your spouse to come up with a settlement that is mutually fair and equitable.

- **Divorce attorney.** You and your spouse each hire your own attorney whose goal is to represent you and get all they can from the other party, working entirely for your benefit. Attorneys have different styles; a litigator will be eager to go to court and fight versus a negotiator, who will do their best to negotiate a fair settlement and avoid a court trial.

- **Pro se.** If your divorce is uncontested and you have no children and few assets to separate, you can represent yourself in the divorce proceedings. You will be responsible for filling out and filing all the correct forms on time and showing up for court appearances prepared. If you are in a contested divorce, though, you should hire professional help.

Pros and Cons of Pro Se Divorce

Pro se divorce (*representing yourself*) is much more common today than it used to be. It's now estimated that in more than 60 percent of divorce proceedings, at least one party is self-represented. In some places, the courts have improved with regard to helping those who wish to represent themselves by providing centers for family law matters, staffed by clerks who help people fill out and file the correct forms. The clerks can't give you legal advice, but they will help you work your way through the procedural rules. Some states have the forms and instructions online, and you can also buy lots of do-it-yourself materials. If you and your spouse both choose to self-represent, you will save a lot of time and money.

Pro Se Divorce Checklist

Here are the typical conditions that are required to be a good candidate for a pro se divorce:

☐ Agree to a no-fault, uncontested divorce

☐ File in a jurisdiction with a summary or simplified divorce procedure

- [ ] Short-term marriage where both spouses work, and assets and liabilities are easily distributed or assigned

- [ ] Division of the marital estate—assets and liabilities—easily agreed upon

- [ ] Do not expect a settlement from each other

- [ ] Agree to waive the right of appeal

- [ ] Can cooperate with each other without emotion

- [ ] Agree to all custody, visitation, and support arrangements

- [ ] Agree on division of assets and property

Pros of Pro Se Divorce

Often an uncontested divorce is the best solution for everyone. These are some of the advantages of a pro se divorce:

- **Cost of the divorce.** Attorneys provide a valuable service, but they cost a lot of money. Making the decision to represent yourselves will dramatically cut the incurred costs. This can be especially important in instances where a lack of finances is an issue.

- **Eased tensions between the parties.** Having the ability to speak directly with your ex, rather than through a lawyer, is likely to ease the tension of the divorce proceedings. This is, of course, predicated on if you and your ex can work together. If you can, then this is likely to ensure a quick and beneficial outcome for all parties.

Cons of Pro Se Divorce

As with any situation, although there may be pros, there are likely to be some cons as well. In the case of pro se divorce, these may include:

- **Development of a contested divorce.** You may set out with the best intentions, but if you and your spouse can't agree on how to proceed, you may end up getting lawyers and courts involved. Worse, you'll likely be starting out on the wrong foot after having gone through heated, but failed, negotiations on your own.

- **Lack of experience.** Attorneys cost a lot because they spend a lot of time studying and learning the law. They have an understanding of the statutes that may apply to your case and access to resources to resolve the often-complex issues that may arise in developing a settlement agreement.

- **Paperwork.** Even if you don't need a lawyer, you'll still have plenty of legal paperwork to get through in a pro se divorce. This paperwork is extremely important as it details your rights and outlines the settlement that impacts your future for years to come. Untrained eyes can miss key details and end up agreeing to a settlement that isn't fair.

- **Emotions.** Attorneys and mediators provide an emotional distance to the proceedings that can work in your favor. A pro se divorce that starts well can turn ugly and become emotionally taxing, which may result in one party agreeing to a bad settlement out of a desire to just get it all over with.

Mediators versus Lawyers

If you can come to an agreement on property division, child and marital support, and custody without outside help, terrific; you win an uncontested divorce! Unfortunately, given the emotions surrounding divorce, this can often be difficult. This is where bringing in a trained third party to facilitate the negotiations can be helpful.

Why You Should Choose a Mediator

Beyond the enormous amount of money you can save, there are many advantages to using a mediator. Let's look at some of the reasons mediation has such a high success rate.

- **You are in control.** Rather than trusting lawyers and judges to make decisions that will affect you and your children for years to come, you maintain control of the process and negotiations.

- **You don't have to go by what the law would say when it comes to your family and property.** In mediation, you have the ability to work out the visitation schedules, custody agreement, and even property division the way you want to. If a court would order half of your spouse's pension to you at age 60 but you would rather keep the house, you are free to try to reach an agreement that would be equitable for both. You have the freedom to be creative and find solutions that work best for both of you.

- **Court is stressful.** The stress involved with a trial is extreme. Someone else is making decisions for yourself and your family. On the other hand, mediation is informal and unintimidating. You control when you meet, who is there, and how much help you get from advisors. Additionally, it is private, so you avoid the public drama of a divorce trial.

- **Legal advice is still an option.** Mediators will provide legal information so that you can make informed decisions even though they won't give you legal advice because they are neutral. If you wish to hire a lawyer to be sure your rights are protected and to give you legal advice, you may do that as well.

- **Less anger.** When attorneys do the talking for you, conflicts tend to escalate. But with mediation, you are talking directly to each other instead of through a third party. A mediator is there to help you communicate effectively and keep you focused on the future, not the past. You are in a neutral setting where each can voice their concerns and desires and where resentment and misunderstandings can be eased and maybe even understood.

- **You may not end up enemies.** Going to trial pits you against each other and almost always ends up with angry feelings on both sides. When you remain in control of your outcome through mediation, you are more likely to feel satisfied with the results and not be bitter.

- **You'll save thousands of dollars.** There's no two ways about it: even if you hire consulting attorneys to help you with mediation, the entire process will cost you much less than a contested divorce with a trial.

The best way to find a mediator is through personal recommendations from someone whose judgment you trust. Lawyers, therapists, financial advisors, or spiritual advisors are a good place to start. If you can't find personal referrals, you can search mediate.com or nolo.com.

When You Shouldn't Choose a Mediator

If both parties are on board, mediation can be a wonderful method to employ during a divorce process, but it can also prove to be a disaster in some situations. If one of you doesn't want a divorce or you're unable to be civil with each other and lack the flexibility to compromise, mediation may not be for you. A few signs that mediation may not be as effective for your divorce journey include the following:

Unknown assets. The two parties don't know the value of assets in the marriage. This may include things such as lacking accurate knowledge of your spouse's income, retirement or pension plans, or value of any owned business.

Parties unable to communicate. If you are not talking, don't think the mediation sessions will change things. The mediator is not a counselor but a conflict resolution specialist whose job it is to help the two of you address specific issues and come to a resolution. If you are not able to communicate civilly, there is not much the mediator can do.

Extreme anger. If you are harboring extreme anger or emotions, mediation probably won't work.

One-sided desire to divorce. If one of you doesn't want this divorce, it doesn't stand a chance.

Belief that there is mediator bias. If you feel the mediator is siding with your spouse, you should stop the process. When one of you has lost confidence in the process, it is time for both of you to retain a lawyer.

Lack of attorney-client privilege. Mediators do not have attorney-client privileges, so that means anything you tell the mediator can later come out in court. If you have secrets that may come out in mediation and may impact you in court, you may not want mediation.

Simplicity does not necessitate complication. If you have a simple case where there are no disputes, you may wish to go straight to an attorney and have them put it in writing. Remember that mediation is for resolving an issue where there is conflict.

Mediation and Safety

If you are intimidated by your spouse or have been a victim of bullying or emotional/physical abuse, you may not want to mediate because they might try to manipulate or control you in the same way. Getting an attorney would be a better alternative to protect your rights. Additionally, if there is alcohol or drug abuse involved, you should be sure they are in a recovery program before considering mediation. If you feel you or your children are in danger, you should make safety your top priority. Develop an escape plan in case you and your family need to leave on a moment's notice and talk to an attorney as soon as you can.

Leaving an abusive spouse statistically increases your risk of harm, but there are ways to do it safely. Contact a local agency that works with victims of domestic violence. They will walk you through how to move forward, so follow their advice. Often your local domestic violence agency can help you to attain a Domestic Violence Protection Order, which is a court order that may grant you temporary custody of your children, order your spouse to leave your home or have no contact with you, and set up child and spousal support. These statutes protect same-sex couples, too, and can also be enacted as final protective orders that include visitation and custody, child and spousal support, and legal fees and costs. You may file for a protection order on your own, but using an attorney is a better path, as you will be required to show proof of past abuse for the court to issue the order.

Trial Attorney

Many of my clients have started the process convinced that they will have a perfectly civil divorce only to see it all go downhill when it comes to finances. This is the point where I suggest that they learn more about what a contested divorce looks like and perhaps reconsider hiring that pit bull attorney. Often, they will return to negotiations with a renewed sense of purpose after seeing how much it will cost them in time, money, and stress to fight it out in court. Most of the time, **the cost of going to court just isn't worth it**.

That said, there are times when using the courts is the only way to move forward. When one isn't willing to compromise on issues that you both feel strongly about, such as the primary income earner being unwilling to consider a reasonable amount of support, one being a poor influence on the kids due to violence or substance abuse and unwilling to concede custody, or you know they are lying about their worth, these are questions that might require judicial review to resolve. Just remember, when you choose this route, you will be bound by whatever the judge decides. Before you make this decision, ask yourself whether it's **absolutely necessary**. Are you really concerned about the issue or just mad at your spouse? This is not the time to be vindictive; you will have to live with the decision for a long time.

How to Choose a Lawyer

The best place to find a good lawyer is through the recommendation of people you know and trust who may have been through a situation like your own. Another option would be to look online at sites like avvo.com that have other attorneys rate their professional colleagues. No matter how you find them, you will want to then go to the State Bar Association website to see if they have been disciplined and to confirm their education and experience.

You will want to set up an appointment to interview your top three choices and find one that you feel most comfortable with. Some will charge for this initial consultation, while others will talk to you for free. You should feel comfortable talking with the person, as they will be privy to your personal information and you will be relying on them to have your best interest at heart.

Some questions to ask a potential attorney:

- How long have you been in practice?

- How long have you been practicing family law?

- Do you handle other kinds of cases?

- Who else in your office will be working on my case? Under what circumstances will someone else be working on my case? What will the charges for that person be?

- Do you or a staff member return calls and messages within 24 hours?

- How many divorce cases have you brought to trial?

- Do you go to mediation?

- Do you encourage people to mediate?

- Are you certified in family law?

- Do you know the judges and courts in the county where my case would be heard?

- Do you know my spouse's lawyer?

- What do you think is the likely outcome of the custody dispute (or support or property dispute) that I have?

- What do you think about arbitration?

- How much do you think this will cost in attorney fees?

- Have you ever been disciplined by the state bar?

- Have I forgotten to ask anything? What else can you tell me about yourself and your practice?

What Does a Lawyer Cost?

A contested divorce will cost you a lot of money. Almost all divorce attorneys will ask you to pay a "retainer," or deposit, when you hire them. This will act as your first payment toward the fees that you will owe as the case moves along. The amount of the retainer is normally based on their hourly fee; almost all attorneys charge by the hour. If an attorney asks for $10,000 up front and they charge $250 an hour, that will last 40 hours. That's a relatively short amount of time in legal work. The retainer goes into a trust account, and they will draw on it as the case progresses. You will get an itemized monthly bill and, believe me, they will let you know when it gets low. They often charge for the time it takes to read an email from you and certainly for any phone calls with you. You will be surprised at all the fees they have that you never thought about.

Should your case go to trial, you can expect your **attorney fees to run anywhere from $20,000 to $150,000.** A one-day trial with no expert witnesses can easily cost in the tens of thousands of dollars, and a more complex one will run into the six-figure realm. Then there's the chance you could end up paying your spouse's legal fees, in addition to your own, should the judge determine that you have the higher income and ability to do so.

Having learned about the alternatives available to you other than a contested divorce fought out in front of a judge, I hope you will seriously consider putting aside your anger and ego and trying to work out a settlement without using the courts to hash it out. It's better for all involved and keeps more money between you and your spouse instead of the attorneys.

What to Do If You Can't Afford a Lawyer

Money provides a tremendous advantage in a divorce, which can be a significant liability to anyone who was a stay-at-home partner supporting a family instead of pursuing a career. Suddenly a divorce is upon them, and they have no job or no significant source of income to pay for the legal expertise they'll need to secure their future. If you're heading into a divorce against an ex who has much deeper pockets, what do you do?

Enter **pendente lite,** a legal maneuver that, among other things, allows your attorney to sue your ex up front for the anticipated legal fees. You will still have to pay a lawyer something up front, typically the costs associated with this hearing. But if there is a wide enough gap between your income and your ex's income, then a judge can order them to pay your legal fees in order to ensure a fair trial.

You should also consider the type of divorce you're heading into. If you can't afford a trial lawyer but are still on good terms with your ex, it may be possible to resolve things through mediation. It's a much cheaper, much faster solution. You also have the right to represent yourself at trial, but that is almost never a good idea. The stakes are too high, and an efficient lawyer will run circles around you in a courtroom.

Legal aid may be available in your area, but as in all things, you get what you pay for. An inexperienced lawyer may be fine for a basic, amicable divorce, but if your ex is actively hiding assets and giving signals that there will be a bitter court battle, you will need to lawyer up. And that may mean figuring out how to get the courts to understand why you need help paying for it.

Collaborative Divorce

Collaborative divorce is a method in which you both hire attorneys who assist you in negotiating a settlement through a series of meetings both separately and all together. These professionals are trained as collaborative attorneys and may sometimes request that other professionals be brought in, such as child custody specialists or accountants. Normally you, your spouse, and your attorneys will sign an agreement that requires the attorneys withdraw and not represent you should the collaboration effort fail and you end up in divorce court. At that point you would have to find an adversarial attorney. If you can come to an agreement, you will go before a judge for the final agreement. It is a simple uncontested legal procedure at this point that won't require further litigation or trial.

CHAPTER THREE

What's Mine, Yours, and Ours

Before the judge will grant your divorce, you must divide up the marital property. You have two options here: you can work together to divvy it up or go to court and ask the judge to do it for you.

In a **community property state,** the court will assume that any assets or debts accrued while you were married belong equally to each of you. If you brought property with you to the marriage, or you acquired it alone during your relationship, you'll ask the court to award it to you as separate property.

Equitable distribution states are different in that the court will divide marital property fairly between the spouses, but this doesn't necessarily mean a 50/50 split. They will categorize the property as marital or separate first, and then the judge will make awards to either spouse. Separate property will need to have proof of ownership with receipts, witnesses, or other evidence.

Debt is included in the property division of a divorce, and you will most likely have to split any joint debt acquired during the marriage such as a mortgage, car loan, or tax debt. If a credit card is in your name only and you never used it for marital purposes like groceries, you may be solely responsible for what is owed on it.

Take note here that a court can assign debt to either spouse; however, **it can't change the contract you have with the credit card company**. So, if your spouse is assigned the debt and doesn't pay it, the credit card company can come after you next. If you don't want your credit score to be affected, you will need to pay it and ask the court for reimbursement from your spouse later.

To start the process, each spouse should create a list of assets and debts and identify which spouse should receive what. When you're both finished, you can compare lists and hopefully work together to resolve it by compromising and trading. Transparency and honesty are key here, as is being flexible and able to compromise.

Both must identify all assets that they acquired throughout the marriage, including bank accounts, insurance policies, vehicles, retirements, pensions, real estate, recreational vehicles, and anything that holds value. The worst thing is to agree on a property settlement and then find out the other spouse didn't disclose everything. If that happens, you can ask the judge to reopen your case and reevaluate the property division, which may cost the spouse the asset, and they can be fined by the court as well if the judge believes they did it intentionally.

An Even Split

Tammy and Leonard had teenage children and had been equal partners in a small business together for 25 years. They also had some real estate worth about $4 million.

Tammy had come to the agonizing decision that she wanted a divorce and decided to try talking to Mark, who worked as a collaborative attorney. During her initial consultation, Mark told her about the collaborative divorce process and her other options for divorce such as trial, arbitration, and mediation.

She wanted to avoid court and all the expense and ugliness that went with it, so Mark suggested that she talk to her husband and see if he would talk to attorneys who also worked in collaborative law. Leonard did so, and after learning about the various court and non-court options, he also wanted to use the collaborative process.

Once they had made that decision and hired their attorneys, they focused on their children. The youngest teenager had recently had a strained relationship with one of the parents, and both parents were worried about the impact the divorce would have on her, but for different reasons. Because of this issue, the parents didn't agree about how they should share time with their daughter when they separated.

The collaborative attorneys recommended the husband and wife hire a child specialist who would meet individually with each parent to understand their concerns and meet with the teenage daughter and the daughter's therapist. The child specialist then went to a collaborative conference with the parents and their attorneys. At the conference, she talked about what their daughter was feeling as a result of the divorce and gave helpful strategies the parents could use to help her through it. The child specialist acted as the daughter's voice when they began discussing custody plans so that her needs were considered. With their daughter's best interests at heart, they were able to come up with a custody plan they both agreed could work.

They met every few weeks with their attorneys to work on dividing their marital estate, and the concerns of each became evident. Tammy wanted autonomy by cutting ties with the business and being bought out by Leonard. There were enough assets in the marital estate to allow for this, but the assets were in non-income-producing real estate. Leonard thought they should hold the properties for future development rather than selling them now for the settlement. If they didn't sell the properties, though, Tammy would have no investment income to replace the income she had been receiving from the business.

They hired a financial advisor through the collaborative process who would value the business and help them find financial options for dividing the assets and providing the income needs of separate households. After several meetings with the attorneys and financial advisor, they agreed to a buyout price and structure that allowed them to delay selling their real estate holdings so they could get the highest sales price; instead, Leonard would pay Tammy monthly payments to replace her lost income until they sold those properties. The financial advisor determined the amount of those monthly payments, and he worked with each of them to figure out their living expenses and make sure the payments would cover Tammy's expenses without creating a shortfall for Leonard. The payments were credited against Tammy's share of the business and taken care of when the land was sold.

After these agreements were made, the attorneys wrote up a formal Marital Settlement Agreement and Property Settlement. In the final collaborative meeting, the attorneys went through the agreement on a large monitor, made final edits and printed the agreement, and the couple signed. Though they were sad, they were also relieved that so much of the conflict they had been experiencing for years was coming to an end and that they had saved themselves the pain and expense of a court battle.

What's Everything Worth?

From houses to bathroom towels, the thought of valuing everything you own might be overwhelming, but **everything you own must be accounted for when you divorce**. What you owned before the marriage and consider your separate property should be identified, and that which was acquired after the marriage much be defined. In most states, you get to keep what you had before the marriage, and everything that came into the marriage afterward will be divided between you through either community property or equitable distribution.

This chapter will give you the basics on how to inventory your assets and debts and explain how they might be divided by a judge if you can't come to an agreement and must go to court. It's easier to do the dividing yourselves because you will each have things that are more important to you, so keep this in mind and be prepared to compromise.

The **initial disclosure form** that you each filed with the divorce petition and the other's response should be helpful in finding much of the information you need. If your divorce is uncontested and you can settle out of court, this might be as much information as you need. But if you're headed for court, you'll soon learn the word "discovery" from your lawyer, which is the formal process used to get the information from your spouse.

Additionally, you might need to hire a financial specialist to put a value on certain assets such as pensions and retirements. Because pensions are for the future, a specialist called an actuary is hired to put a value on the pension as of the date of separation. Another specialist you may use is an appraiser to put a value on your home, any other real estate, or vacation homes.

If you suspect your spouse is hiding assets or money, you can hire a forensic accountant to follow the money and see if it is all accounted for. Sometimes failing to disclose can be unintentional, such as when one forgets about a certificate of deposit that was purchased long ago. But other times it may be deliberate, and you need to find them to make solid and fair decisions on the property division. If they have been withdrawing money from places such as brokerage accounts or equity in your home in preparation for the divorce, it's not right or fair.

Red flag! If your spouse's income looks lower than usual, there's a chance they have asked their employer to increase their withholdings so their paycheck looks lower. This will affect support amounts and result in a large tax refund the next year. You can get around this dodge by NOT giving up your right to future tax refunds. If your spouse is reluctant to share financial information with you or resists your efforts to gather information, be alert and hire a forensic accountant.

Remember, unlike money, physical items depreciate. Spending serious time and money going to court over an item you could replace for a fraction of the cost makes no sense. Keep in mind that trying to win will only leave you both as losers in the long run and make the attorneys winners.

Creating Your List of Assets

If you followed the financial checklist in chapter 1, you will have a head start on valuing your assets. You've probably already split up your household items and come to an agreement on clothes, jewelry, personal items, and gifts if you're separated. Remember, it's often cheaper to replace an item than to fight about it in court.

Next, you'll need to deal with assets that have changing values like stocks, bonds, mutual funds, and other financial items. If they are too complicated to evenly split, you may need to hire a financial specialist to help you.

Before sitting down to negotiate, have the following items in front of you:

☐ Personal income tax returns for the past three to five years

☐ Business income tax returns for three to five years

☐ Proof of your current income (pay stubs) for three to five years

☐ Proof of your spouse's income (pay stubs) for three to five years

☐ Bank and investment statements (three years): checking, savings, money market and CDs, and anything from your financial advisor

☐ IRA, SEP, 401(k), and any other retirement plan statements

☐ Pension statements

☐ Health, homeowner, auto, and life insurance policies

☐ Trusts, wills, and living wills

☐ Power of attorney for both of you

☐ Stock option statements

☐ Mortgage statements for all properties

☐ Loan documents on any loans like car, home equity, or consumer loans

☐ Utility bills and any other bills

☐ Appraisal documents on any separate property

☐ List of property or valuables you owned prior to the marriage

☐ List of contents in a safe-deposit box

- ☐ Copies of any recorded debts

- ☐ List of sport or event tickets, frequent flyer miles, accrued vacation statements, etc.

- ☐ Your list of household items (with values)

Knowing what you want when you start negotiating, such as the house, mutual funds, art, or any items that you are emotionally attached to, is important. Try to detach yourself from material things and think with your head instead of emotion.

Ask yourself if you need to be able to access money from an investment account or if it's fine to wait until long-term bonds mature. A financial planner is the professional to bring on board if you need help in considering your long-term goals.

Professional Appraisals First

Professional appraisals will be needed on anything of value that may be a point of contention. Some items should be appraised professionally, like jewelry and antiques. Boats, RVs, and cars can usually be researched online and a blue book (trade-in) value determined. A house is normally a couple's largest asset and should be appraised, but possibly not until you are close to negotiating so you get the most accurate selling price. Finally, a CPA will be needed to help you value your financial assets if they include a business, stock options, or retirements and pensions.

If you own a small business, you are in for a tougher time in assessing the value and dividing it. Trying to keep it running while this upheaval is happening can be a challenge in itself, but figuring out how to continue operations (especially if you both work there) can be tough. This is where having rules about what can and can't happen during the separation can be helpful. Valuing a small business is tricky. If one is keeping the business and the other is selling their half or exchanging it for other assets, both want different valuations.

The factors that go into deciding the value of a small business may include:

- ☐ What a comparable business sold for recently

- ☐ Assets and inventory

- ☐ Debts and obligations

- ☐ Potential income

- ☐ Terms of payment, meaning a buyer who can pay cash usually gets a lower price

Even if the business was owned prior to the marriage, it will most likely still be considered a marital asset because time and attention was given to it during the marriage. Getting a valuation from a lawyer, accountant, or business appraiser will help you determine how to divide it up.

Fair Market Value

The courts will use **fair market value** in determining the value of an item. That means the cash equivalent of the item on the street market, so whatever you could get for it if you tried to sell it right now. You might be disappointed at the low value of your furniture, but the courts consider used furniture worth as low as ten cents on the dollar from what the purchase price was, so don't put a lot of energy into fighting for the furniture when it may be cheaper to replace it. To find the value of your furniture, try looking up items on Craigslist.com to see if you can find similar items and what they are selling for. Your other items might be found by doing a search on eBay, and if you can't find them there, try taking the price of the item when new and depreciating it by how long you believe the life of the item would be. The key here is to be able to find values that are somewhat close to what the item would be worth in the eyes of the court before you sit down to negotiate. One couple divided items up with the wife taking all the furniture and household items and the husband taking everything with a motor except her car. He got the two four-wheelers, the boat, and even the lawn mower and blower. It worked for them and kept them out of court.

Equitable Distribution versus Community Property

In court, property will be divided based on the laws where you live. **There are two kinds of states: community property and equitable division (noncommunity property).** The community property states are Alaska, Arizona, California, Idaho, Louisiana, Nevada, New Mexico, Texas, Washington, and Wisconsin.

A community property state says that property is owned equally during the marriage and should be divided equally in divorce. However, there are exceptions to this. In California, Louisiana, and New Mexico, the property is always divided equally, but in Idaho, Nevada, and Wisconsin, a judge starts with this presumption, and then a spouse who disagrees can argue their case and try to persuade the judge differently. In Arizona, Washington, Texas, and New Mexico, the courts try to give each spouse a fair share of the community property. "Fair" usually means equal value or something close to it.

Dividing equally doesn't have to mean that every single asset will be split in half; it means the court tries to make sure each spouse ends up with an equal total value when the dividing is done. Given that, it doesn't necessarily mean there won't be arguments about who gets what, but to the court it is more about the value of the items and what is separate or community property.

In an equitable distribution (noncommunity property) state, you own the income you earn while you are married. If you have property in your own name, you own it and have the right to manage it while you are married, whether you both paid for it or it was a gift to you both. However, equitable division in divorce means the judge tries to divide the property equitably (in a fair way), but not necessarily equally. Judges won't simply give all the property to either spouse based on whose name is on the title. For instance, if a woman stayed home and raised the kids while her husband worked, under equitable distribution her work would have held no value. If he got to keep all the money at divorce, her contribution to the family would have had no value.

Equitable distribution is meant to see that each spouse gets a fair share of the property, whether or not their name is on the title. It means that each spouse contributes to the family, acquiring property and income whether both names are on the title or not. It can also sometimes mean that you will be awarded property instead of support, especially if you were married for a long time. Judges may prefer to award property instead of support to try to give the spouse a standard of living somewhat comparable to that of their marriage but without continuing the ties between spouses.

Negotiation of Who Gets What

When negotiating your divorce, you'll be splitting decisions into two categories: affordable and acceptable. The best strategy is to look for a compromise that balances the two, making sure that solutions are legal and clearly understood. As you work through the divorce process, it is important to remember that it's not just about putting price tags on everything. To make the negotiating process go more smoothly, you should consider the following:

- What is the least that you are willing to give, and what is the least that you are willing to give up?

- What is the most that you are willing to give, and what is the most that you are willing to give up?

- What is the absolute minimum that you both are willing to accept?

As you reach an agreement on each issue, I urge you to make that topic closed, so as not to keep revisiting areas and issues. Revisiting decisions means reversing your momentum. This is a long and complex process, and you need to **keep moving forward**. Every agreement can change in light of new information or extenuating circumstances, but trying to renegotiate settled issues, especially late in the process, will undermine good faith agreements going forward and may damage the progress made so far.

It's not easy negotiating for your future welfare and for the future welfare of your family. Controlling your emotions is key to successful negotiation. With this in mind, I offer the following tips that I hope will help you through the negotiation process of your divorce journey.

Tip 1: Don't Draw Lines in the Sand

Try not to be stubborn. Fixating on one position rather than focusing on the end goal is akin to drawing a line in the sand and is not actually negotiating. Consider approaching negotiations with an open mind and understand that both sides will need to compromise. Begin the negotiations in the right frame of mind with the goal being a settlement that you can both live with.

For instance, if you determine you will not pay your ex a penny more than $1,800 a month in alimony, they may take the position that they won't settle for anything less than $2,400 a month in alimony. This results in a stalemate on the issue of alimony, which could result in your entire divorce proceedings becoming a costly and painful court conflict.

Tip 2: Bullying the Other Party Isn't Productive

Using a bullying tactic during negotiations almost always fails. Equally useless is the "my-way-or-the-highway" attitude. Both tactics can be the quickest and most expensive route to the courtroom.

Tip 3: Salvage Your Relationship

Although you are divorcing, relationships matter. If you have children, this is especially important. You will need to co-parent with the other parent even after the children are grown, so as difficult as it may be, try to preserve a semblance of a healthy relationship throughout the negotiating process. The marriage may be ending, but your parenting relationship is not.

Tip 4: Practice Empathy

Try to understand, and this will help for you to be understood. If you don't make an effort to understand where your spouse is coming from, it is highly likely that you will not be able to negotiate successfully. The other party's perception may not necessarily be your reality, but it is theirs. Being able to understand the other person's triggers and perceptions can help you to arrive at creative solutions as you work on reaching an agreement. Many times, individuals are willing to sacrifice financial gain in order to have an emotional need satisfied. Recognize that if you are able to put yourself in the other side's shoes and understand their perceptions and emotions, it can result in a better deal for you.

Tip 5: Maintain Control of Your Emotions

Do your best to recognize that it is very important for you to control your emotions while navigating the divorce journey, and try not to make emotional decisions. In some situations, this is akin to putting on your poker face, and doing so will likely serve you well. On the other hand, if you don't control your emotions and engage in emotional decision making or emotional outbursts, the other party will learn what your trigger is, and that's like showing your cards. This could result in some difficulty in negotiations that could have otherwise been avoided. Failing to maintain your emotions can also lead to a breakdown in divorce negotiations and lead to an increase of costs and time.

Tip 6: Fair Agreements Require All the Facts

It is important that both sides know all the facts and have the same information regarding assets, property, and debts. You'll also need a clear understanding of how the law applies to each of them. If you have engaged the services of an attorney, be sure that your attorney has reviewed your spouse's financial disclosure form and applied the law in determining what is fair for you.

Tip 7: Focus on the Problem, Not the Person

If you are able to focus on the issue at hand rather than focusing on the person who you are divorcing or being divorced from, you will find it infinitely more valuable to the process. Emotions will be intense during this process, so do your best to separate the problem that you face from the person with whom you are negotiating or disagreeing. If you find that you are beginning to focus on the person rather than the problem, try your best to bring the focus back to the negotiation.

Tip 8: Both Sides Benefit from a Win-Win

It is important to recognize that one dollar to your spouse is not necessarily the equivalent of one less dollar to you. Do your best to search for the win-win result where both of you come out of the divorce process with what you each view as a fair agreement. Knowing the other party's end goals makes it easier to reach a win-win resolution.

Debt Is an Asset, Too

Congratulations if you have no debts and only share assets, but that's rare. In most cases, you'll need to divide up your debt just like you do your assets, starting with determining what debt is community and what is separate. Use the same general rules for dividing debt that you used for assets.

Community property states will hold you both responsible for any debt incurred during the marriage whether you both signed for it or not. In an **equitable distribution state**, debts in your spouse's name will be considered theirs alone, but if your spouse took on a debt without your knowledge and put your name on it, you will normally still be held responsible with these exceptions: if your spouse used credit to buy things that only they would use and you knew nothing about in anticipation of the divorce.

For example, if your spouse makes a large purchase without your knowledge on a credit card, a judge will look at all the circumstances like whether you or your kids benefited from the debt incurred and whether you consented to it. If your spouse buys expensive furniture for your child's new dorm room, you could be held liable for this, though, because it benefits the child. That said, if your spouse buys sporting equipment that only they will use or expensive clothing that only they would use, those debts might be considered separate by the court.

It is important to note here that even if a credit card debt is assigned to the other side in your divorce settlement, a credit card company can and will hold both parties responsible. If the other side doesn't make a payment on a credit card even though your divorce decree says they are supposed to, be assured the credit card company can and will come after you! They will still consider it a joint debt if both your names are on the credit card application, and your divorce decree doesn't nullify the initial contract you signed with the credit card company. You would have to make the payment to save your credit from being damaged and then seek remedy in family court.

Student loans are a special kind of debt. If you took out a student loan before you were married, it will stay with you after the marriage. If you were using joint funds to pay it off during the marriage, many states will consider these payments to be a gift, yet other states will make you repay them through marital property division. No matter what, the remainder of the student loan will remain your responsibility. However, say you took out a student loan during your marriage; it is normally considered a joint responsibility. If you used the loan to pay for educational expenses and then got divorced before you could use your education to benefit the family, the court will give you full responsibility for the remaining balance.

Paying off your joint debt is the easiest way to handle it, so **if you have equity in your home or other available assets, selling them to pay off your debt is the easiest way to move forward** with certainty and protection of your credit. It also allows you both to make a fresh start with no lingering issues. Even if one spouse is buying out the interest of the other spouse, there will most likely be a refinancing, and the buyout price can take the debt into account.

Bankruptcy

Though financial problems may have been one of the causes of your divorce, getting divorced doesn't necessarily make them go away. You and your spouse will need to resolve your financial issues before you can finalize your divorce.

Though bankruptcy is one way to solve your debt problems, you should carefully consider its repercussions. Bankruptcy, in many cases, will eliminate your debt, other than student loans, with no tax consequences. However, it will also stay on your public record and credit report for ten years. You may have to disclose your bankruptcy on job and loan applications, and it will affect your ability to get new credit. At the very least, you will have to pay a very high interest rate when financing because a bankruptcy now makes you a high risk.

Child and spousal support can't be written off in a bankruptcy. If your spouse files for bankruptcy, you are normally better off cooperating with the bankruptcy than fighting it because in most cases the court will take your interests into account if it will affect you.

There are two types of bankruptcy, and it would help for you to know the difference between them.

- **Chapter 7 bankruptcy.** Known as a *liquidation bankruptcy*, Chapter 7 is where the debtor (person who filed the bankruptcy) gets to keep a small amount of property, but everything else is sold and the money gained is used to pay off the debt. Debts that aren't paid in full are then discharged (wiped out). Your income must be under a certain level, and you can't include student loans, money owed to the government like back taxes, or money for child or spousal support.

- **Chapter 13 bankruptcy.** Also known as a *reorganization bankruptcy*, the debtor will come up with a plan for paying back some or most of their debt over a three- to five-year period. The repayment plan can provide for anywhere between 10 to 100 percent of the debt depending on how much income the debtor has left over to live on after the payment. If they complete the payment plan, the remaining debt is discharged (wiped out). People often will use a Chapter 13 bankruptcy when their income is too high to qualify for a Chapter 7. One advantage of a Chapter 13 is if you are behind in your house payments; you may be able to pay the deficiency over the three to five years rather than all at once. The biggest disadvantage is should you lose your job or be unable to make a payment; you will be kicked out of the bankruptcy and be responsible for your debts again as well as the interest accrued while you were in the bankruptcy process.

With either form of bankruptcy, when you file an "automatic stay" comes into play. This means that all creditors that you list in your bankruptcy are forbidden from trying to collect the money owed during the payment time and after it is fully discharged. Remember, though that domestic support obligations and student loans are not dischargeable, so they will continue to exist even after the bankruptcy is done.

Property settlements are not normally included in the support obligations, so they can be discharged in bankruptcy. To protect yourself from losing your settlement share if your ex files a bankruptcy after the divorce, you can tie all the assets you are promised in the settlement to another asset such as a retirement account that the bankruptcy court won't typically touch. For instance, if you're promised a large portion of the equity from your house in the settlement, and then your spouse files a bankruptcy and allows the house to go into foreclosure or back to the bank, the amount you would have been awarded in equity would be taken from their retirement account. This can get legally complicated, but having it written in your settlement agreement allows you some sort of protection and may deter your ex from filing a bankruptcy to get out of paying their debts. Sometimes a court will consider a spouse's promise to pay off debts in your settlement to be a support obligation and thus non-dischargeable, and some states will consider attorney's fees as non-dischargeable as well. If you think your spouse may file a bankruptcy after the divorce, you would be smart to accept higher alimony and less property settlement so that your future payments aren't jeopardized.

You will want to see a bankruptcy attorney of your own as soon as your ex files a bankruptcy to make sure your rights are protected. If your spouse files a Chapter 7 after the divorce, whatever money they owe you through the settlement might possibly be wiped out. However, if they file a Chapter 13, whatever debt your former spouse owes you at the end of their three- to five-year time period can be wiped out. You can put a lien on real estate prior to the bankruptcy, though, and you might get lucky. Liens are considered a secured debt and must be paid in full as part of a Chapter 13.

If your spouse agreed to take over joint debts as part of the settlement and then files a bankruptcy, the creditors are likely to come after you. In a Chapter 13, creditors can come after you if your name is also on the contract. You can try talking to the creditors who are coming after you and explaining the situation, but they are not bound to your divorce settlement; they have a contract with both your names on it. You can either try to negotiate a lower settlement with them, pay the debt, or take a hit on your credit rating when not paying the debt. If you choose to pay off the debt yourself, you can sue your spouse for reimbursement; however, if they have filed a bankruptcy, there is little chance you will collect anything. Your attorney may choose to file as a creditor in your bankruptcy, and you will want to be sure that this doesn't jeopardize your ability to go back to family court should your support need a modification. It is illegal for a creditor to pursue a debtor after they file a bankruptcy.

Should you file for bankruptcy before or after the divorce? If you get along well enough to work together through filing for joint bankruptcy before you file for divorce, this could simplify the process and wipe out all joint debts for both of you. That said, it can also slow down your divorce by making you wait until the bankruptcy is settled before you can divide up assets.

Filing for a bankruptcy jointly before the divorce can make the property settlement process much less complicated because there is less debt to divide between you. Additionally, you won't have to worry about whether the other is or isn't paying their bills (in order to protect your own credit) after the divorce is settled.

Legal Fees: Need-Based versus Sanctioned

Contested divorces can be a very expensive proposition. With spouses arguing over everything from alimony and child support to who gets custody of the family pet, attorney's fees can skyrocket. In fact, the monthly legal invoices are what finally cause many couples to settle down, put animosity aside, and try to peaceably resolve their differences. Sometimes one spouse will ask the other to pay both sides' divorce-related legal fees, and how that is decided by the court involves many considerations.

Family law courts in most states are authorized to order one spouse to contribute to the other spouse's attorney's fees, especially in cases where there is a big difference in their incomes. Judges can order a higher-earning spouse to cover all or part of their ex's legal fees.

In some states the policy on attorney fee awards is that if one spouse can afford to pay for both sides' fees while the other spouse would have to proceed without a lawyer unless they have some contribution, then an order for fees will be considered both necessary and fair in order to level the legal playing field between the parties.

In some cases, courts will order an award of attorney's fees to a lower-earning spouse because it's clear the higher-earning spouse will be able to recover financially after the divorce is finalized.

In situations where neither spouse is making a sizable income but there's still an earnings difference, decisions on attorney's fees are more likely to vary from state to state. In some states, if the lower-earning spouse will at some point have access to marital assets that can be used to generate funds to pay those fees, such as bank accounts, stocks, or a 401(k) retirement plan, the court may be less likely to grant an award for legal fees.

If a cash-poor spouse needs money up front for a lawyer, the court may sometimes let them use some of the marital property to cover costs until the assets are finally split up, on the understanding that their ex will get reimbursed for the difference.

However, with dual-income families, judges are less likely to order one spouse to pay the other's fees. Today it's probably less likely than in the past that one spouse is completely reliant on the other for money. When faced with spouses who each earn about the same income, courts are generally inclined to let each spouse bear the burden of his or her own attorney's fees.

Judges don't like it when spouses behave badly during the divorce process; not only does bad behavior drive up attorney's fees (for both sides), it also prolongs the divorce process, causes unnecessary stress, and wastes valuable court time and resources.

When a spouse intentionally disrupts the court process and drives up the cost of litigation, a judge may be inclined to grant the other spouse's request for attorney's fees as a penalty for that conduct.

Some common examples of disruptive tactics include:

- Constantly filing motions (formal requests) about trivial matters with the court

- Ignoring court orders (usually until threatened with contempt of court)

- Delaying providing requested information to the other spouse (such as financial documents)

- Failing to attend mediation sessions, hearings, or any other court-ordered program

If your spouse (or their lawyer) engages in this type of behavior, it will invariably lead to you incurring much higher attorney's fees. Your lawyer will have to respond to these frivolous motions or file their own motions to force compliance with court orders and keep going back to court for rescheduled hearings.

For example, if your spouse intentionally disrupts the court process and drives up the cost of litigation, a judge may decide that it's unfair for you to pay for their conduct and could order them to pay a portion (or all) of your attorney's fees as a penalty.

CHAPTER FOUR

The Parenting Plan

Breaking the news to your kids is hard, and it's even harder watching them go through the emotional turmoil that will follow. Figuring out the custody and support arrangements is probably the hardest part of the divorce process. A commitment to keep the children's welfare as the priority during this process may help you both keep your emotions in check and work harder to settle things amicably.

When it comes to custody and support, you have two options: you can either work it out together or you can have the court decide for you based on what the judge thinks is best for your children. You should be able to agree that it's best for your kids if you lessen the conflict they witness. Keeping them out of court will help reduce uncertainty about their own future.

In this chapter we'll walk through developing a parenting plan that will work for both of you and still put the children first. Here is another opportunity to take the high road. As long as there is no physical or verbal abuse in either house, you will need to support your children's relationship with the other parent. Now is the time to put away any anger that you might have toward them and work together to come up with an agreement that is the least disruptive to your children. Remember that you chose who your children's parents would be, and they only have two parents. Hurting the other parent only hurts your children in the long run, so try to graciously work together to pound out a parenting plan that will work for everyone.

Children of Divorce

Worrying about the damage a divorce will do to our children is always the most difficult part of splitting up. Will they be damaged for life? Will they be angry or lose their faith in marriage? Is this a selfish decision as a parent?

Following is an editorial written by Elizabeth Rembert, a Senior News Editor of *The Daily Nebraskan*, who is a grown child of divorce. Her perspective is through the eyes of a child who has grown up and ruminated on how her parents' divorce affected her and shows there can be positives for your child in the grand scheme of things.

Dear Reader,

Like many people, my parents are divorced. My childhood has the typical story of a messy separation: nasty words in terrible fights and way too much grown-up stress and responsibilities put on ten-year-old me.

Despite the bad memories, I wouldn't trade it for anything.

I won't deny that I've used my "broken family" as material for scholarship application essays, but I've come to resent society's lens on divorce—that separation is the worst possible outcome and stems from two people's failures to just "work it out." No good marriage ends in divorce, and I see it as a liberation for two people and their children to find better ways to be happy.

I constantly see articles and tweets glorifying the "We were born in a time when if something was broken you would fix it" mantra for marriage, and it makes my skin crawl. Divorce is more complicated than just falling back in love, and suggesting that hard work and endurance are the only answers is dangerous.

The idea that staying together is the only successful way through a marriage's hardships undermines the growth that divorce can bring. I've seen this growth in my own parents, and in my own life. Eleven years after the divorce, my dad is eight years sober and my mom is flourishing past her insecurities. If my family were still together in our small farmhouse, I don't see how they could have worked past each other to reach their best selves.

Both have remarried, and the new relationships have shown me a healthy picture of love that I don't think I could have seen in their marriage to each other.

And yet my mom told me that shortly after my parents began the divorce process, an old woman from our tiny, rural Nebraskan community approached her to warn her of the affects her decision could have on my siblings and me.

"I hear you're getting a divorce," she said to my mom. She and my mother had something in common: both of their husbands were addicted to alcohol, but my mom had opted for divorce and she had stayed with her husband.

"Well, I just wanted to let you know that my kids always thanked me for staying with their dad," she told my mom.

This decision might have worked for her, but I'll speak for myself. I would never have wanted my parents to stay together. I've seen them grow outside of their marriage, and both have made me so proud by getting out of their unhealthy relationship and choosing happiness over appearances and pride.

I'm not saying that divorce is a goal. No one aims for separation and it's not on my bucket list, but my experiences taught me how empowering divorce can be for families. Instead of a "broken" home, mine became a new beginning.

With love,
Elizabeth Rembert
Senior News Editor, Daily Nebraskan

Creating calm, secure, and loving homes for your children may help them develop in ways that may not have happened without the divorce experience. Following are some ways it can have a positive influence on your children's lives:

- **They grow up to be more resilient and adaptable.** Divorce forces change through moving, career changes, and even partners. Less money in a single-parent household often requires a parent to work when they had been able to stay home before, and this may mean the children need to chip in more on chores or they might come home to an empty home after school and need to take care of themselves. Teach them to take pride in their resilience as they naturally become more self-sufficient

- **They grow closer to siblings.** You may notice they grow closer to their siblings as they navigate the emotions that go with divorce. When they must move between your homes, the one constant may be their siblings.

- **They develop empathy toward others.** It's during the most difficult times that our heart grows the most. Children who have lived through loss and pain learn to look at others with more understanding and empathy.

- **You are able to give them individual attention.** Your child might spend more quality time with each parent than before because when you only have your children part-time, it allows you to handle other responsibilities when they are with the other parent. You might also get counseling for your child during this time, and they can learn skills that will help them later in life.

Children of Same-Sex Marriage

Until gay couples have the same legal equality as heterosexual couples, they remain second-class citizens in many divorce advocates' eyes. In the *United States v. Windsor* decision, Justice Kennedy repeatedly used the word "dignity"; divorce is part and parcel of the dignity that needs to be afforded to relationship—the dignity not only to get into one but to get out of one.

This is demonstrated in the case of Lillian and Sharon, who lived in Massachusetts when gay marriage was legalized. They made the decision to tie the knot at the encouragement of their parents and twin sons in 2004. Having a small ceremony in their backyard, they thought it was the right decision for their family at the time.

Two years later, it became apparent that marrying might have been a hasty decision in the excitement of the moment of legalization. They filed for divorce in 2006.

Because one had borne the children and the other had adopted them, they were able to avoid a bitter custody battle. Both names were on the birth certificate, so they didn't have to deal with the parental rights problems where federal and state laws often collide. For gay couples, when either one person is the adoptive parent or one carries the child and the other is not named on the birth certificate, the biological parent can sometimes close the other parent out of the child's life. Likewise, the other parent can just walk away with no responsibility for visitation or support.

Four years later, Lillian remarried, and this time she had a prenuptial agreement. This was a good idea since this marriage also failed to work. She was protected from paying spousal support and losing part of her estate. She still is resentful, however, that the expectations seem higher for gay couples than opposite-sex marriages.

She notes that though she has been able to avoid legal issues that many gay couples face, she feels her divorces reinforce the conservative view that gay couples aren't able to maintain healthy monogamous relationships. Many gay couples feel the pressure to have a perfect marriage since they are creating a new tradition and often feel unwarranted guilt or shame if their marriage doesn't work.

The Parenting Plan

Family court will ask you to work together to make a comprehensive parenting plan that includes a custody agreement, visitation schedule, and conflict resolution guidelines.

If you can't come up with one together, you can each submit one separately or the court will appoint a third party to do one for you, but doing your own lets you tailor it to your own family by adding "provisions" for specific issues. If you can't work on it together, submitting separate parenting plans is allowed, and **the judge will choose based on the one that will be the most developmentally beneficial for the children in the long run**.

Remember that a parenting plan is a legal document that spells out how you will share the responsibilities and costs of raising your children. It should be flexible yet realistic and detailed enough to be useful in establishing the rules. Make it appropriate for the current ages of your children, keeping in mind that you can modify it in the future as the children grow and their needs change.

A carefully developed parenting plan is not only for the court but also to clarify the expectations in your new co-parenting arrangement. Used thoughtfully, it will be a guide and help you both avoid confusion while laying the foundation for a successful co-parenting relationship.

Parenting Time Schedule

Consider your children's ages as you develop your schedule; for example, babies and toddlers need more frequent time with each parent, while teenagers need flexible schedules that fit with their social lives and activities. Remember that you **may need to change your parenting plan multiple times** as your child grows and their needs and activities change. Different temperaments do better with different schedules, so if your child is easygoing, you'll have more flexibility in choosing a schedule than if they need more consistency or struggle with change. You'll want to choose your schedule accordingly.

These tips are about school-age children (6 to 12) and might help make your parenting plan more effective:

- Children can handle longer separations from each parent once they are in school and start spending time with friends and doing activities.

- School-age children understand time and routine, so give them a calendar showing the parenting schedule and other activities.

- Normally, school-age children are more independent and comfortable with having two homes.

- Different parenting styles are more easily adjusted to by school-age children.

- A creative parenting plan can be adapted to because children become more flexible as they grow older.

- Both parents should support and encourage activities outside the home.

- School-age kids should be able to talk privately on the phone to the other parent, and this should be annotated in your parenting plan.

- When both parents get involved in the child's schooling, they do better. Both parents should have a chance to help with homework, attend conferences, and attend school activities.

- Older children will form opinions and want input on the schedule, and this should be welcomed, but the final decision should remain with the parents.

Medical and Health Care

Research the custody guidelines in your state to determine if it requires medical insurance as a component of the parenting plan. You will likely find that most courts will want to see how health care will be handled. Recognizing that each divorce is unique, you may desire that your parenting plan include provisions beyond those required by your state. If health insurance is not available through either of your employers, you may be required to purchase private insurance and split the cost or find a way to work it out.

Some suggestions for items to include in your plan regarding medical expenses include:

- The associated cost of health insurance. Write in that the costs will be paid by each party as follows: (%) by Party 1, (%) by Party 2.

- Both parties will provide and be given a copy of involved children's health insurance cards.

- Medical, optical, dental, and mental health expenses, co-payments, and deductibles that are not covered by insurance will be paid by both parties as follows: (%) by Party 1, (%) by Party 2.

- If a party to the divorce incurs a child-related medical expense while with them, they will provide the other party with copies of all health care–related bills within ___ days of receiving the bill. (I suggest 30 days.)

- If one party takes initiative to make payment for expenses or incurred copayment expenses that necessitated payment at the time of service, the other party should agree to reimburse the party that incurred the expense or made the payment, for the agreed-upon percentage of the bill, within ___ days of receipt of the bill. (I suggest 30 days.)

- Whether or not health care is a covered insurance, if possible, approval from both parties will be received in advance, in writing or email or by order of the court, in any case where it would result in an out-of-pocket expense of over _____ to either party. (I suggest $100.)

Education and Activities

Each state's guidelines are unique, so like health insurance, do your research; however, this is a list of the information that most courts will want pertaining to your child's future education. Whether you have joint or sole physical and legal custody may impact how you fill this out. You may want to include other provisions that **keep both parents informed and involved**.

School-Related Information

- The name, address, telephone number, and school district of the school that the child(ren) attend.

- How will future decisions be made regarding where the child(ren) attend(s) school?

- Which parent's address will be used for school registration?

- Make an agreement upon how information such as how academic progress reports, school meetings, parent conferences, field-trip permissions, school photo permissions (and payments), and access to parent portals for school websites will be handled.

School Participation

- Which parent can be part of school activities like sporting events, proms, plays, concerts, or academic visits like parent-teacher conferences or open houses?

- Each parent is required to inform the other parent when their child is late, absent, or removed from school early.

- Each parent agrees their child will attend school until graduation, unless special circumstances such as illness, court order, or academic probation preclude this.

- Each parent must put studying and schoolwork first, even if it means less time to do other activities. Additionally, parents must agree to inform each other about any assignments and provide details on when and how they are to be done.

Academic Notification and Student Record Access

- You should make an agreement on which parent (or both) will be given access to associated academic records.

- Who will be listed as the emergency contact?

- There should be agreement that both parents are responsible for providing their contact information to the school.

- Each parent should provide the school with a signed medical release form.

- A copy of the parenting arrangement, including time-sharing details, will be filed with the school.

Extracurricular Activities

- Make an agreement on how both parties will discuss or decide upon extracurricular activities and in an agreeable time frame prior to enrollment of the child in the activity.

- There should be a clause that both parents must mutually agree upon extracurricular activities. This is also true in cases where an activity might create overlaps in scheduling.

- It is also wise to include a clause about which parent is permitted to attend extracurricular events (possibly both).

Parenting Guidelines

As with other areas, I urge you to research your state custody guidelines to find out the specific guidelines regarding your parenting plan. It is typical for your plan to allow for additional provisions, beyond the state requirements, so that it works for your unique situation and allows you both to resolve any issues that may be a point of conflict or confusion.

Provisions that you might choose to include in your parenting plan include:

Discipline

- Each parent is responsible for disciplining the children while in their care. If a significant disciplinary problem arises, there should be an agreed-upon process or communication that will occur whereby one parent will contact the other parent to arrive at a solution.

- Neither parent will permit a third party to inflict physical punishment or discipline of any kind to the child(ren).

- Unless mutually agreed upon, no discipline shall be taken that overlaps, changes, or minimizes the agreed-upon parenting schedule or where it would deprive the other parent of their scheduled time with the children.

Child Rearing

- Parents both agree to teach the children to respect and obey teachers, the law, and authority.

- While at their home, the parent will supervise the children except when they are at school or taking part in extracurricular activities or are otherwise under the care of a competent person.

Food, Diet, and Home

- Each parent's home will provide life essentials such as water, heat, and electricity.

- The child will be provided properly balanced and healthy meals while in the custody or care of each parent.

Religion and Faith

- There will be a mutual agreement of the parents as to what (if any) religion the child will receive instruction.

Tobacco, Alcohol, and Drugs

- Make an agreement that either parent has the ability to deny the other parent access to the child(ren) if it is determined that the parent is under the influence of drugs or alcohol to a point that would inhibit their ability to provide for proper care and supervision of the child, present a threat, or impede the safety or well-being of the child(ren).

- Make an agreement that neither parent will use dangerous or otherwise restricted drugs (except by prescription) within (an agreed-upon time frame) prior to or during periods of providing care or supervision of the child(ren).

- The parents agree not to expose the child(ren) to secondhand smoke (of any type) or vaping fumes while in the home or care of either parent.

Significant Others

- Both parents agree not to have romantic partners spend the night (out of wedlock) while the children are at their home.

- Unless married, all romantic relationships will be kept discreet with the children's interest first and foremost.

- Neither parent will confuse the children by using the term "stepmother" or "stepfather" until the parents are legally married.

Childcare

I advise that any plan contain details that explain how the determination will be made about where any child will go in the case that childcare is necessary while the parents work. It should also detail how the parents will decide on who will provide and who will pay for said childcare.

Make sure to detail **the right of first option**, which means that if either parent is unavailable, the other parent is given the chance to provide childcare first instead of a third-party like a grandparent or day care.

Parent Communication

Throughout the divorce process and after the divorce is finalized, it will be important for both parents to be able to communicate with regards to the care and well-being of their children. What is of paramount concern is that such communication is done in a manner that is minimally impacting upon the child. That is to say that **parents should not be prone to arguments and outbursts in front of the child** or to bad-mouthing the other party in the presence of the child. Mature, constructive communication is necessary and appropriate to best support the child's emotional and physical well-being.

Suggestions that might help with your co-parenting strategy include:

Ground Rules

- Make an agreement to communicate regarding the child's schooling, dress codes, and physical and emotional health.

- Identify the primary method(s) whereby the parties will engage in communication.

- Make an agreement not to use the child as a messenger and agree to communicate directly with one another.

- Agree not talk about one another or about the child in the presence of the child.

Dispute Resolution

- In the event that the parties are unable to reach a mutually agreeable decision pertaining to the child's health or well-being, the parents agree to seek assistance from a licensed third party or a professional mediator/arbitrator.

- In the event dispute resolution becomes necessary, each party will pay the cost of resolution as follows: (%) Party 1, (%) Party 2

- A clause about how the dispute resolution process will be instituted and how the other party will be notified should be included. Suggestions for notification include: written request, certified mail, etc.

Parenting Plan Revision

- It is suggested that parents determine a specific time frame for when/how often they will meet to review the parenting plan and make any changes that are necessary.

- Terms and conditions of the parenting plan can be supplemented or changed as the needs of the child and/or parents change. Changes will be in writing, signed and dated by both parents, and each parent will keep a copy.

- Either parent may request a change to the parenting time schedule or parenting plan in writing, and the other parent has 14 days to respond.

Traveling and Relocating

The plan should clearly state how much vacation time per year is granted to each parent, and it should also include conditions about traveling and, if necessary, relocating with the child. Some points to address include:

- Prior to traveling with the child, each parent agrees to provide the other parent with the following: advance notice of (number of) days, travel itinerary and ticket details, and contact information at travel destination.

- Each parent must have written permission from the other parent or an order from a court of law to take the child out of the child's identified home state, including during agreed-upon schedule and parenting time, unless of an emergency nature.

- Note whether parents may travel internationally with their child.

- Neither parent will apply for a child's passport without permission of the court or without the permission of the other parent.

Additional Considerations

As with the aforementioned areas, you will want to explore what is required (or suggested) within your state's guidelines. In addition, you may wish to **include provisions to tailor your plan to meet your family's unique needs**. Considerations when making additional provisions may include:

- Which parent (if any) had primary care of the child prior to the separation?

- Individual needs and important issues associated with your child.

- Strengths and weaknesses of each parent.

- The personal desire of each parent to share the parenting responsibilities.

- The relationship of the children with their siblings.

- Are your children old enough to have their desires considered when making decisions?

- How will you inform and explain the details of your parenting plan to your child?

Additionally, you should consider that:

- The court won't accept your plan unless it complies with the state's guidelines and laws.

- Your child's age should be considered when developing your plan.

- If either parent is in the military, you'll need to provide consideration for the possibility of deployments.

- Only one state can have primary jurisdiction, meaning parents who live in different states must follow the laws of one state only.

- In the event that there are multiple children, a split custody arrangement is possible that would allow for parents to have custody over different children at different times.

Revising the Plan

Your plan must contain information about how you will revise the plan as it becomes necessary. You should have a process for reviewing and revising the plan as well as how to resolve disagreements about revisions.

Thinking ahead may save you from having to revise it. Here are some tips:

- For the court to accept your plan, it needs to follow state laws and custody guidelines.

- Your plan should be appropriate for your child's age and developmental needs.

- In military households, certain military provisions can be included in the plan.

- If both parents are separated by long distance, you can include travel provisions in the plan.

- Your first plan can be temporary to give you time to develop a permanent custody plan once the separation is finished.

- Your plan can also change as your children get older and have different needs.

Types of Child Custody

Legal custody means the right to make decisions about a child's general welfare (education, medical, etc.), whereas **physical custody** means where they physically live.

Joint physical custody (shared physical custody) means the child will spend a significant amount of time living with each parent, and both have equal responsibility to physically care for them. It doesn't necessarily mean they will have equal time with the child, just substantial and frequent time. Joint custody works best when you live close enough to work logistically and you both want to be very involved in the children's lives.

A creative new idea that is working well for some joint-custody families is called "nesting," where there is one home where the children live and the parents move in and out rather than the children. This alternative provides continuity and security in the children's lives but works only when parents can communicate with each other comfortably.

The alternative to joint physical custody is **sole physical custody,** where the child lives with one parent and the other has regular visits with the child.

Sole physical custody might be necessary when:

- You both agree that sole custody is in your child's best interest.

- One parent travels a lot for work, making it difficult for the children to live with them.

- One home is more appropriate due to the child's age.

- Parents live far apart and agree to a long-distance custody schedule.

- One parent has substance abuse issues or is mentally unstable.

- One of the parents has been absent from the child's life or has a history of abuse or neglect toward the child (which may necessitate supervised visits).

Calculating Child Support

Most states have a formula for calculating the child support required of each parent, based upon the income of each. It is my suggestion that you and your spouse look this formula up online and attempt to figure it out yourselves rather than spending money to go to court and argue about it. In most cases, the court will agree with you if you both agree and if it appears equitable.

While income is certainly a primary consideration factor, there exist some additional factors that may be taken into consideration in calculating each parent's child support. These include:

- Whether a new partner or spouse is contributing to household expenses for one of the parents.

- Whether either parent receives bonuses, incentive pay, severance, or other lump-sum payments that make their income less predictable.

- Ages of the children.

- If a parent is having deductions taken from a paycheck to cover union dues.

- Day-care costs.

- Health insurance costs.

- If a parent has any children from a previous relationship and pays child support or alimony to another family.

- If a parent receives child support or alimony from a previous marriage.

If you need help supporting your children while you are going through the divorce process, this can be done through a **temporary child support** arrangement while the divorce is pending. If you can agree to this yourselves, you can save a lot in court fees. Just research "estimating child support for your family," and there are calculators that will help you. Additionally, you will want to look at your expenses and figure out how much you will need to keep your head above water. If you can't come to an agreement, you can go to mediation or to court, and they will award **pendente lite,** or temporary support, orders while the divorce is pending.

Child support should be taken very seriously. Late payments are subject to annual interest fees as high as 10 percent, and failure to pay can cause the court to seize assets to collect payment or, in extreme cases, send the offending party to jail. However, child support and visitation are two separate things. Even if your ex is late on payments, you cannot refuse visitation or refuse payments if your ex is not honoring visitation agreements.

CHAPTER FIVE

Settlement Agreements Explained

Once you have reached an agreement on the major issues, a written contract called a *marital settlement agreement* (MSA) is attached to the final divorce decree. The terms of the marital settlement agreement are legally binding and enforceable obligations for both of you. The main points that must be included in a marital settlement agreement include:

- The agreement was entered into freely and voluntarily by both parties

- Legal and physical custody agreement

- Schedule for visitation

- Child support

- The amount of spousal support or a statement that explains why it has been waived

- Distribution of all assets including personal finances, debts, retirement accounts, and marital residence(s)

The **final step in the divorce process** is a *prove up* hearing. This is a short hearing where the judge will review the MSA and ask if each party to the divorce understands everything in it. They'll confirm that everyone voluntarily entered the agreement and was not under duress. They may possibly also ask you some brief questions about the agreement and then sign the divorce decree to make the divorce final.

The Value of Agreement

The marital settlement agreement isn't just important in getting the judge's approval; it will also be important in providing **a road map for your future** if there are conflicts or confusion or should it need modifications. It's an important document, so take your time in getting it done and be careful when checking the details before you finalize it.

Whether you choose to settle through mediation, arbitration, or pretrial negotiating, you can add provisions to the agreement to tailor it to your own unique situation and concerns. It is when you go to trial and have the court make these decisions for you that you give up this flexibility.

It's critical that you understand the implications of settling out of court; however, any provisions that you add to the agreement can come back to haunt you if they are not detailed or clear enough and the court needs to interpret them at a later date when there is a conflict. You should each have a divorce or family law attorney review the document and make sure that you fully understand it and how the laws apply to it. They will also notify you of possible ramifications of specific parts of the agreement and assess whether it seems fair to both of you and covers your concerns.

Adding unique provisions to the settlement agreement are a benefit to settling things without a trial. Your situation is known best by you, so handing the decisions over to a judge can be a gamble with the future of you, your spouse, and your family.

Sometimes the added provisions in marital settlement agreements, especially when it comes to finances, alimony, and assets, can do more than laws alone. Child support and custody, however, normally vary by state and county and have more rigid guidelines.

These additions must be agreed to and understood by both parties, though, because once your divorce is finalized, they are enforceable even if you didn't fully understand their ramifications.

The following scenario shows why it is so important to have an attorney review your agreement before signing it. Legal counsel during mediation, or at least prior to signing the marital settlement agreement, will explain the ramifications of the MSA and any provisions. Even if your divorce is amicable, it is just the smart thing to do.

Some states have **cohabitation laws,** which mean that anytime two adults enter a mutually financially beneficial relationship, even without being married, the courts may have grounds to modify alimony agreements. Cohabitation can play a large role after divorce since a spouse who is recognized as cohabiting will often no longer require financial support in the eyes of the law.

A divorcing couple added a special provision regarding how future cohabitation would affect their support agreement. The definition of cohabitation in their agreement included any situation where one lived with a family member, which went beyond the New Jersey cohabitation laws that only covered romantic relationships.

It had major consequences. The wife moved in with her sister after the divorce was final in an effort to save money. When her ex found out, he immediately filed to modify their spousal support agreement. This request would normally have been denied, but due to the provisions in the MSA, the court ruled that the husband no longer had to pay alimony to his wife even though she testified that she did not understand the specific terms in the MSA when she signed it.

When the decision was appealed, the appellate division confirmed the trial court's ruling because "there were no compelling reasons to depart from the clear, unambiguous, and mutually understood terms of the MSA. The agreement was voluntary, knowing and consensual, and the alimony-termination event upon cohabitation was fair under the circumstances of the case."

Both parties are agreeing to the terms of the divorce in your marital settlement agreement. When you present your MSA to the court, they will look at the financial and property division but will cover most closely the portion that has to do with the children. They want to make sure that you understand and agree on the issues related to the best interests of your children. If the judge doesn't feel your agreement is putting the children first, they can set it aside and not issue your divorce decree.

Once the agreement is finalized in the court, it is possible, but very difficult, to have it changed or set aside. This should underline the importance of seeking the advice of an attorney before signing it because if the language is clear, it will usually stand up in court in the future.

How Do I Know If My Settlement Is Fair?

When negotiating your divorce settlement, remember that *equal* and *fair* are two different things. Fair does not necessarily mean a 50/50 split. So what is fair may not mean what is equal. In the eyes of the court, "equity" means what is fair to each party in their individual situation. No one gets everything they believe they are entitled to, so be prepared and be willing to allow for compromise.

During the process of reaching a negotiated divorce settlement, the court will take multiple factors into consideration like your standard of living, length of marriage, and long-term needs when determining what they think is fair. Again, most times it is best to decide this between yourselves with the help of a mediator or attorneys if needed because you know what is important to each of you and can tailor the settlement to your specific wants and needs.

No-Fault Divorce

All states now have some form of no-fault (irreconcilable differences) grounds for divorce. This means the person asking for divorce doesn't have to prove their spouse did anything wrong. (It used to be required that you provide proof with traditional fault grounds of cruelty, adultery, desertion, or confinement in prison.) You now only need an irreconcilable breakdown in the marriage that has lasted for at least six months for a no-fault divorce. No-fault divorces are not only less contentious, here are some other reasons they are now an option in all 50 states:

- **They establish an amicable tone.** How a divorce starts out will set the tone for the rest of the proceedings and future co-parenting relationship. While one person may indeed be the main cause of the divorce, starting the process by blaming will only make things more adversarial.
- **They keep legal fees down.** Going to court to resolve differences is expensive and emotionally draining. Settling outside of court is always the best way to keep legal fees down.
- **You can focus on needs, not who's at fault.** Blaming won't change the past or make anything better going forward. Your energy is better focused on dividing assets and custody matters.
- **There is no incentive to make false allegations.** False allegations have no reward, so there is less pressure to prove the other is at fault.
- **They ease emotional burden on children.** Children feel stress during a divorce, but hearing that one parent ruined the marriage can make a child feel like they should take sides.
- **They are faster.** No-fault divorce is normally less adversarial than fault divorce, so it may speed up the process of getting on with life and establishing a co-parenting relationship.

How to File the Settlement Agreement

Ninety to 95 percent of divorces will settle without going to trial because the spouses have been able to agree on the marital settlement agreement either between themselves or through their attorneys or mediator. Once this is done, they (or their attorneys) then present this MSA to the family court where they filed the initial petition. If the judge agrees to the terms in it, they enter a decree that reflects the terms of the MSA. If the agreement is not obviously unfair, the judge will usually agree to the terms in it. **The court may use certain language on the decree such as "merged," "survived," or "incorporated." These terms have special meanings and affect whether an agreement can be modified or enforced.**

If a settlement agreement is *incorporated*, it becomes part of the divorce decree. If it is not incorporated, then it cannot be enforced through contempt of court proceedings.

A divorce agreement is *merged* into a judgment when it becomes part of the judgment and can later be changed by the court. The court that granted the divorce continues to have jurisdiction over the order and can modify the judgment. The judgment might say that the agreement is "merged" or "incorporated and merged," which means the agreement basically turns into the decree. The agreement is transformed into the judgment and has no separate legal significance.

Both parties can petition the court to enforce the agreement or to ask the court to hold the other party in contempt if they are not complying with the court's order. Typically, the spouse who wants to modify a merged agreement must show a significant change of circumstances that wasn't present when the initial decree was issued.

If the court incorporates and merges the agreement, it can only enforce provisions that it would have had the authority to order originally. If the agreement has a provision that the court wouldn't have had the power to order, the court can't enforce this portion of the order later. If there are provisions that the family court doesn't have authority over, the party that wants to enforce it would have to take it to civil court under breach of contract. This method is sometimes preferred for unconventional provisions that are part of the decree, such as post-majority (over 18) support for adult children. While the court may lack the authority to order such support, people are generally free to enter into contracts for it at their own will.

The divorce court will always continue to have jurisdiction to modify a child-support award. Child support can be modified by the court, and this power cannot be restricted simply by the parents making an agreement to set child support at a certain amount. Child support is ordered to protect the children's interests, and the parents cannot bargain with these rights.

CHAPTER SIX

If It Goes to Trial

Most divorces are settled out of court, but not *all* divorces. Some couples can't agree on all the issues and end up going to trial. In this chapter we'll delve deeper into what you'll need to prepare for it. If you can't settle before the trial begins, the judge's job is to issue a ruling that resolves unsettled disputes. **You both will be required to abide by their judgment.** You can only appeal or seek a modification if you can show a significant change of circumstances to get a hearing, and then you can fight to have the ruling overturned. Whether you hire an attorney or try to do it yourself, trials take a lot of time and money, so **reconsider settlement one last time** before trial starts.

If you settle on most issues, but a few are still in dispute, then you can take only those specific issues to court. For example, should you reach an agreement about property division but can't agree on child custody, only the custody issue needs to go to trial. Even though judges have years of experience, no one understands your situation better than you. That's why family law attorneys will try to get you to come to an agreement if it's at all possible.

Putting a stranger in charge of dismantling your family structure after only a few hours or days of testimony can drain you emotionally. Judges aren't there to be "fair," they are there to make decisions they believe will be equitable in the long run. Judges aren't always perfect, and the most deserving or honest party doesn't always get what they hoped for. Consider your court case to be about finances and custody, not about emotions and blame. How "fair" you play the game doesn't necessarily mean you win.

Trial and Error

Ninety-five percent of divorces settle out of court, so don't be surprised if your attorney approaches you with a settlement offer prior to trial. **Remember, half of people who go to court will lose.** There's not really going to be a winner, either, because neither side is ever totally happy with the outcome. It's likely any hopes of an amicable relationship may be destroyed in the process, too. How you behaved during the marriage doesn't influence the decision, nor does behavior during the separation (unless it involves the children.)

Good attorneys cost money—a lot of it—and can substantially change the outcome of your case. The person with the most money often comes away happier. Even so, when you win, you could lose a lot due to how much you spent on your good attorney to get there.

Mediation, collaboration, or having your attorneys work toward settlement gets harder if your ex is an abuser, narcissist, or high-conflict individual. These personality types will probably find it difficult to compromise at any cost. If there is a history of bullying or violence, fair negotiations are nearly impossible, and you may end up heading straight toward a court trial.

You also need to realize that **the system works slowly,** and it takes a long time to get to trial. Even then, the judge doesn't necessarily rule right at the end of the trial. Sometimes a judge keeps a case under advisement for weeks or even months.

When they have a final ruling, the judge will fill out a form spelling out the rules of your relationship going forward. These are considered a court order and can be enforced by the court.

When you are preparing for the trial, pretrial discovery procedures are used to collect the information to establish the credibility of the other sides. The plaintiff (person filing) requests information from the defendant to "make known what had been unknown." It can be time-consuming and expensive but is indispensable.

Discovery is required to establish **accurate valuation** so that the marital estate can be divided evenly. Your discovery phase will include:

- Request for financial statements

- Production of official documents

- Answering of written questions (interrogatories)

- Statements made under oath (depositions)

- Subpoena and subpoena *duces tecum* (subpoena of third parties)

- Keeper depositions (subpoena duces tecum)

- Request for admissions (like interrogatories but require yes/no answers)

- Motions for physical and mental examination

- Request to enter land and notices

It can be a difficult phase. Parties often bring emotions into the process, and it involves asking for information from your spouse's side and third parties like mothers, fathers, and siblings as well as corporations and businesses. Following are some procedures the attorneys will use to acquire this information:

Interrogatories. Each side can ask detailed written questions. For example, attorneys may ask if the financial statement or mandatory disclosure is both accurate and complete and get the answer in writing for the record.

Deposition. Each party can ask questions under oath, and the answers are recorded by a court stenographer. The notice of deposition will include a request for all documents that must be brought to the deposition.

Subpoenas. Subpoenas are issued to any person or institution, such as banks or employers, that has financial records that are pertinent to the proceedings.

Actuaries. Actuaries can calculate what pensions and any employment retirement benefits are worth.

Appraisers. Like actuaries, appraisers can calculate the value of a range of assets including businesses, real estate, or collectibles like art and jewelry.

Private investigators. If there is a question about truthfulness, private investigators will try to verify someone's work habits, lifestyle, and personal life if it might impact their finances.

Although very broad discovery requests may be considered burdensome by the court, a request due to a specific purpose for "any and all documents" is not. **In divorce, discovery can include everything a person owns and owes,** like checking and savings accounts, mutual funds, and money market accounts; real estate records that include the marital home and second homes and unimproved land; personal property; automobiles, furnishings, and collections (art, stamps, coins); stocks, bonds, annuities, pensions, and profit sharing; retirement plans; accrued vacation time; medical savings accounts; other valuable personal property; life insurance; season tickets; credit card statements; vehicle loans; mortgages and home equity loans; promissory notes; and student loans and any other debt.

If the other side doesn't cooperate with legitimate discovery requests, the courts can bring sanctions, which are a punishment for bad behavior. Your attorneys will try to work it out between themselves, but if that doesn't work, they can file a *motion to compel* through the court. The court will have a hearing and may sanction the party.

Your Pretrial Checklist

Most of the legal fees are tied to pretrial preparation. Your attorneys gather evidence long before the trial begins to build a case on the issues in dispute and to build support for your preferred outcome.

Usually both parties are deposed, meaning you are asked questions while the answers are recorded by a court reporter. This can take hours and **will be under oath,** so lying is perjury. You will need to bring the documents requested such as mortgage bills, bank statements, business records, emails, and anything that will be relevant, and your ex's side will ask for documents as well. You might need to hire experts who will testify, especially if children are the issue. The issues in conflict will determine the depth of the evidence-gathering process.

Let's discuss the procedures that might be implemented on both sides for the trial preparation. Hopefully you have already gathered many of the documents when you did your initial mandatory disclosures for the original petition for divorce, but more information may still be requested.

Financial Affidavits

A financial affidavit is a net worth statement that gives a detailed financial balance sheet of personal expenses and assets. This is normally a sworn statement filed with the court, so being accurate is very important.

Professional appraisals of property, businesses, and other assets may be secured by the attorneys so that they have current values for a fair division of marital assets. Psychological studies might be requested to confirm that the home environment is adequate if child custody is at issue.

Disclosures

This can be the same disclosures document you used after filing the initial petition for dissolution of marriage. It's a list of all your assets and debts and must be accurate. It will typically look somewhat like this:

Except as otherwise agreed by the parties or ordered by the court, each party must deliver the following documents to the other within 45 days from the date of service of the summons:

(a) The parties' federal and state income tax returns and schedules for the past three (3) years and any non-public, limited partnership and privately held corporate returns for any entity in which either party has an interest together with all supporting documentation for tax returns, including but not limited to W-2s, 1099s, 1098s, K-1s, Schedules C, and Schedules E.

(b) Statements for the past three (3) years for all bank accounts held in the name of either party individually or jointly, or in the name of another person for the benefit of either party or held by either party for the benefit of the parties' minor child(ren).

(c) The four (4) most recent pay stubs from each employer for whom the party worked.

(d) Documentation regarding the cost and nature of available health insurance coverage.

(e) Statements for the past three (3) years for any securities, stocks, bonds, notes or obligations, certificates of deposit owned or held by either party or held by either party for the benefit of the parties' minor child(ren), 401(k) statements, IRA statements, and pension plan state- ments for all accounts listed on the 401(k) financial statement.

(f) Copies of any loan or mortgage applications made, prepared or submitted by either party within the last three (3) years prior to the filing of the complaint for divorce.

(g) Copies of any financial statement and/or statement of assets and liabilities prepared by either party within the last three (3) years prior to the filing of the complaint for divorce.

Review of the Pleadings

Prior to the pretrial conference, the attorneys will review the initial pleadings for both sides to make sure they have everything they asked for and to see whether they need to ask for anything new to be fully prepared for the trial. **They will clarify which issues are going before the court and which ones are not.** Additionally, they will make a list of what relief each side is requesting. It can be several months since they've reviewed the original petition, and this review can be helpful to highlight and flag the relevant portions of the pleadings. When they make their opening statements, you may see the attorneys refer to this list for reference.

Trial Depositions

Depositions can be long, involved, and very exhausting. Lying during a deposition is considered perjury. It will feel like testifying in court, and normally your attorney will be present. The other side's attorney will ask questions and will come very prepared.

The deposition will preserve testimony that may have otherwise been eroded by time. When you testify in a deposition, it's hard to change your story in a trial. A deposition will typically have more open-ended questions where they can glean information that might be helpful in coming to a settlement or at the trial. When testifying at a trial, the questions will be more specific with close-ended questions. Expert witnesses and third-party witnesses may also be deposed. Depositions can be very expensive but extremely helpful.

Exhibit Management

The exhibits and witness lists will all be submitted to the court in the weeks leading up to the trial. They should be organized and include any documents you intend to use or have witnesses review during the trial. This will also be provided to the opposing side's attorney. At the trial, your attorney will introduce the exhibits so they can be accepted by the court.

Trial Preparation

Prior to the day of your trial, your attorney will brief you. You should **show up to the courthouse an hour early** so your attorney can discuss if they have been able to come to any compromises with the other attorney that may make the trial shorter or avoid it all together. **Judges love this.** They'll also tell you to dress nicely; no jeans or T-shirts. They will also tell you how to testify and tell you not to offer any information that isn't requested. They will suggest that you provide short, truthful answers without emotion that stick to the question. Certainly, do not approach or address your ex or their attorney directly because acting irrationally can affect the court's decision.

Witnesses and Depositions

Expert witnesses provide specialized insights on key areas relevant to the divorce. Typically, an expert witness has unique training and skills that cause the court to recognize their testimony as something beyond mere opinion. Before testifying, an attorney **must submit evidence that shows why the witness is an expert in their field**. This frequently includes certification of advanced training or academic degrees.

These are the most common expert witnesses in divorce proceedings:

- **Psychologists and child therapists.** After an evaluation, they often provide testimony regarding what is in the best interests of the child. They can also verify claims of child abuse, an important piece of evidence in contested divorce cases.
- **Real estate and property experts.** When property division is contested, an expert witness with special knowledge in market-value calculation may be necessary. A specialized expert such as an antique dealer, art dealer, or jewelry appraiser might be necessary when valuing property or collections.

- **Financial experts and accountants.** Often used when one party is actively undervaluing assets or income. They can uncover hidden sources of income or accounts that can affect things like property division or child support and alimony.
- **Vocational expert.** They are experts in what a person can potentially earn in a given field. In cases where one partner stayed at home to support the family, a vocational expert can be called in to determine the value of the career that person set aside. This information can have a dramatic impact on the length and amount of alimony.

A witness's deposition is sworn testimony taken outside the court. It is used to gather information as part of the discovery process and may be used at trial in some circumstances. The **deponent** is the witness being deposed.

Since depositions don't directly involve the court, the process is done by your attorney. A deposition will include the deponent, attorneys for both parties, a person qualified to administer the oath, and a court reporter or stenographer to take written transcription or an electronic recording means acceptable to the court.

All parties may question the witness; lawyers are not allowed to coach their clients' testimony, and objections to questions are limited.

Depositions might be considered hearsay and thus inadmissible at trial, but there are three exceptions to this rule: if a person admits to something that is against their best interest, if a witness's testimony in trial contradicts their deposition, or if a witness is unavailable for the trial.

Depositions can also be done with written questions that are submitted in advance, and when the deponent appears, they only have to answer those questions. These are cheaper than oral depositions because the attorneys don't need to attend them with the witness but less useful because there are no follow-up questions. Normally, interrogatories can be used instead of written depositions and achieve the same outcome.

The Divorce Trial Timeline

The petition for dissolution is filed and answered, settlement attempted, discovery done, and finally you are ready to go to trial. There is a light at the end of the tunnel, and you will find an end to this long process. Worn out emotionally and probably financially as well, **you will need all your strength to get through this final phase**. It won't be easy, but know that in the end you will have achieved your goal and be liberated from your marriage.

Here are the steps to the trial once you've finished the discovery and both parties are ready. Either attorney can file a *notice for trial* or *note of issue*, which asks the judge to schedule a trial date. You'll want to do this early because it can take months or more to get a date.

Pretrial Hearing

Though different states and counties conduct their court procedures uniquely, they will usually follow a similar pattern.

Most courts will require a **pretrial conference** to make sure both sides are ready for trial. This conference will set the ground rules for the trial, including the exchanging of trial documents. The filing spouse (plaintiff) will file an "at issue memorandum" when they think both sides are ready for trial, and this tells the judge to go ahead and schedule the pretrial conference.

The judge will want the parties to try to settle by having a pretrial conference or court-ordered mediation to talk through the issues one last time before going to trial. These conferences are a good way to explore solutions that might make a settlement amenable because there will be a judge or mediator there reminding you that neither of you will get everything you want in a trial.

The goal is to arrive at a fair settlement. This is the sweet spot time, about 30 to 60 days before the trial, where both parties might be able to see how much they are about to spend to have the judge make their decisions for them. Often you might see how the judge reacts to different issues and whether that might work in your favor or not. It might make one side more willing to negotiate a last-minute settlement.

If they absolutely can't settle, the judge will finally set a trial date. Most divorce trials are set between 60 to 150 days later.

Opening Statements

At the start of the trial, both parties get an opportunity to give an opening argument to outline the different issues in contention. Both attorneys will briefly touch on the facts and evidence that support the competing outcomes. Your attorney will try to tell a narrative to the judge that allows them to see why you are entitled to what you are requesting. **An opening statement is meant to be brief** and not the time to argue the case, and the judge can cut it short. Your case will be argued during the closing arguments, after your evidence and witness testimony has been fully presented.

Examining Witnesses

After the opening statements, the trial will move straight into examining the witnesses. The petitioner who filed the case (plaintiff) will call their first witnesses. These witnesses will usually be yourself, your spouse, any expert witnesses, and any relevant third-party witnesses such as therapists, teachers, and so on.

Direct Examination

When your own attorney questions you on the stand, it's called direct examination. That is when your attorney will try to get you to tell your story to the judge. The attorney will ask open-ended questions that guide you through the narrative.

It's important during direct and cross-examination that you **keep your cool and don't get emotional**. No matter how angry you are or wronged you feel, this is not the place to tell the judge everything your spouse has done to you. It's understandable that you are upset and want the judge to understand the situation from your side, but **you**

are legally limited to only testifying about the matters that are relevant to your case. If it is a no-fault state like California, you don't need to justify why you are getting divorced, and the judge will not allow you to talk about your spouse's infidelity on the stand; you will be required to stick to the issues.

Cross-Examination

Cross-examination is when the other side asks you questions. They will try to ask you leading questions that will be mostly yes or no answers that probe your direct testimony.

Don't volunteer more information than is necessary to answer the question, simply respond to exactly what was asked. For example, if you are asked what kind of car you have, tell them a Ford (or whatever you drive), but don't expand and tell them you drive a red 2002 Ford with black interior and four doors. Take a minute to think about the question before answering so your attorney can object if they don't think it is relevant or fair.

Closing Argument

Finally, both sides are finished presenting their evidence, the witnesses have been examined, and the exhibits are entered. Each attorney now has an opportunity to sum up their argument, apply it to the law, and present it with the conclusion they are seeking in a neat little package to the judge. This leaves the ball in the court's hands and draws the trial to a conclusion.

Proposed Final Judgments

The conclusion of the trial doesn't necessarily mean you will have a judgment that day. Very often a judge will wait to make their final ruling for days or even weeks while they take all the information both sides have presented under advisement. They often will ask both attorneys to submit final judgments that pretend that they are the judge and write the order that they want the judge to make. These are often submitted in a word-processing document format. If the judge somewhat agrees with your side, they will work off your document to create the final ruling.

The Ruling

After the judge's decision is made and delivered orally or in writing to the parties, a judgment will be typed and approved by the lawyers and court. Sometimes it takes days or weeks. The written judgment is then "entered" on the court records, and a divorce decree is issued.

The **divorce decree is different from a divorce certificate**, and they have different purposes. The state issues the divorce certificate for record-keeping purposes, but the divorce decree is a final, court-enforceable order that resolves all the issues that were part of the divorce. Once signed, the decree will make your divorce final.

Appeals

If one of you disagrees with the ruling, you have 30 days to appeal all or part of the decision through written arguments done by your attorney. They will argue that the judge didn't follow the law in reaching their decision. However, appeals in divorce cases are rarely successful because the judge has a lot of discretion in how to make their ruling. It is more common and successful to deal with changes through modifications.

Modifications, unlike an appeal, don't argue that the judge made a mistake; rather, they say that since the trial your circumstances have changed significantly and that the agreement should be modified to reflect those changes. Note that most states will require a significant change in circumstances in order to even hear the case, though. For example, if you are supposed to pay $5,000 a month in child support and then lose your job, you can ask for a modification to temporarily or permanently lower the child support you are supposed to pay. States and courts determine what constitutes a material or significant change of circumstances differently, so you will want your divorce attorney to tell you what a material or significant change of circumstances looks like in your jurisdiction.

You may think this is the end, but there is much to be done after the judge signs the final decree of divorce. Some of the more common examples include:

- Organizing the quitclaim deeds for the transfer of ownership in houses/real estate property

- Loan refinancing

- Updating insurance policies and retirement accounts with new beneficiaries

- Drafting, reviewing, executing, and filing qualified domestic relations orders (QDROs)

- Transferring titles for automobiles

- Transferring property as directed by the court or agreement

The expense for completing the final transactions is often surprising. Some don't require lawyers but will still cost you. It's important that you budget for these tasks even after the decree is signed.

Unforeseen Issues

Susan and Jolene were the couple you saw out marching for equality, huge advocates for the right to marry, and the ones who danced in the street when that right was given in 2008 by the state of California.

They had been together since the '90s, and after years of waiting, they were finally able to marry in May 2008 when California's Supreme Court ruled that "an individual's sexual orientation—like a person's race or gender—does not constitute a legitimate basis upon which to deny or withhold legal rights." They married the night before

Proposition 8 passed in California several months later, once again banning same-sex marriage. And once again, their status was blurred.

After fighting so hard to have the right to be married, it was most shocking to themselves when they had to admit that no matter what they did, they just weren't working as a married couple. The thought of getting divorced seemed like a betrayal not only of their vows but to their whole movement and cause. There seemed to be higher expectations of gay couples than there were of heterosexual couples just because of the battle they had fought to earn the right to be married.

Because same-sex marriage was relatively new to the scene, the problems with how to fairly divorce were becoming evident. Susan and Jolene had been cohabitating since the '90s but only married since 2008. They had filed for a domestic partnership in 1999 in California and didn't know if that would need to be dissolved separately as well. Was there credit given for all those years that they weren't allowed to be legally married?

Having been divorced from the father of her children in 1983, Susan ruminated on how much more complicated that divorce should have been, yet comparatively, it was simple. This time, though intermingling their lives, Susan and Jolene had kept their property and money separate. That didn't make the divorce much easier, though. Since they moved from California to a state where same-sex marriage wasn't legal, there were all kinds of laws that came under scrutiny for the first time.

After reams of paperwork and court hearings along with thousands of dollars in legal fees, they were finally legally divorced in 2014 when the Supreme Court made marriage equality legal in all states.

As a 50-year activist and even knowing that lesbian couples divorce twice as often as gay men, Susan is often asked if she regrets getting legally married, and she answers a solid yes. But only because by doing so she submitted herself and Jolene to being guinea pigs in an agonizing and devastatingly expensive process from which it takes years to recover. That said, when asked if she would fight for equality again and the right to make a life with a lover and honor that love with marriage, she answered, "Yes, in a heartbeat."

CHAPTER SEVEN

Post-Divorce Issues and Advice

You did it, it's finally over, and you can move on with your life! Sometimes the divorce process can be so absorbing that you don't take the time to consider your future, and when the process is finally over, it can be paralyzing to realize that **the future is here**.

It's important in this new phase to keep looking forward and not back. Here's a helpful saying:

"If you are feeling anxiety, you are thinking too much about the future.

"If you are feeling depressed, you are thinking too much about the past.

"If you are at peace, you are living in the moment with a heart of gratefulness."

You get to build your life the way *you* choose to, so put some quality time into thinking about how you want your world to look now, in a year, and in ten years. If you don't know where you are going, how will you know when you get there?

You can choose to look at your divorce as **a time of loss or a time of opportunity**. Challenge yourself to look at it with a positive mindset that gives you hope. You are in control of your thoughts and self-talk, so take control of them and create the life you were destined to enjoy.

There will be some loose ends to tie up from your divorce, but for the most part, focus on creating your new life. You'll be amazed at the new group of friends you'll find in the community of divorcées. People that have gone through divorce are very empathetic and understanding, so reach out to support groups and make some new friends. It'll give you someone to talk to and inspire you when you see that they have survived just fine.

A New Tomorrow

The only reason I got out of bed for almost a month after my divorce was to take my dog outside. If he had thumbs and could have turned a doorknob, I probably would have stayed in bed all day. After 27 years of marriage and three grown children, I found myself utterly lost. I had always defined myself as a wife and mother first and a career woman second. Married to a man who wanted to be a pilot but had never been in an airplane, I spent my first five years of marriage helping him realize his dream. I then spent the next 20 years raising children while he was off flying for the military and then the airlines. I didn't mind; I loved my life. The kids were great, our home was nice, and we traveled a lot because we didn't have to pay for airline tickets.

I always worked part-time to help, but my main job was raising the kids and keeping the home. Pretty traditional, but I was happy. I kept in shape, tried to be Mother of the Year, and managed to build a good career while being the primary caretaker of our children. We bought and sold several homes along the way, and I'd like to think that my decorating on a shoestring budget helped to save a lot of money.

After 25 years, I found out he was having an affair, and it was a downhill slide from there. Once the trust was gone, especially given his career as a pilot, we just couldn't get it back. My divorce was in a no-fault state, and because I had proven I could make money, I was given a few thousand dollars in alimony and lost my health insurance, too. This was during the 2008 recession, so when our home sold, we lost all the equity we had in it. In other words, I was closing in on 50 years old and starting over with almost nothing.

During my divorce, my sister's 19-year-old son had a diving accident and became a quadriplegic. It was a tragedy that changed all their lives forever. Then my 42-year-old sister-in-law was diagnosed with a terminal brain tumor. At Christmas that year, my brother toasted, "Someone parked in God's parking place, and they need to move their car. Let's hope we never have another year like this."

Though devastating to me, my divorce just didn't seem so bad considering my nephew's accident and sister-in-law's illness (she died the next year). Their problems brought my own into perspective and jolted me into reality; my kids were healthy, I was healthy, and the rest didn't matter.

A friend suggested I make a dream board and put pictures on it of all the things I liked and wanted in my life. What an eye-opening experience that was for me. Suddenly I realized that I hated living in the winter cold with snow, slush, and gray cloudy days. I wanted palm trees in my life, and there was nothing keeping me from realizing that dream. I could live anywhere I wanted; I was liberated.

I also realized that I missed having the chatter and laughter of kids in my life. Mine had grown up, and the youngest was in college while the other two were already college grads. I missed just being around those young minds.

When I stood back and looked at that dream board day after day, I realized that there were no pictures of men on it. Wondering why this was, I had to do some soul searching. I finally admitted to myself that I had never lived on my own and was relishing the thought of it. I had gone from my parents' house to college to being married. All my life I had been answering to others for everything I did and relying on others to keep me afloat.

I needed to prove to myself that I could make it on my own before I could bring a healthy me into a new relationship. I wanted to know that if I got into a relationship, it was because I wanted to, not because I needed to either emotionally or financially.

Well, here I am 10 years later with an established career that I love, living in California, and happily single and dating. I've had the opportunity to work with A-list celebrities, fly on private jets, work with families I adore, and write a book. I've moved three times, completely replaced all my old furniture, and paid cash for the Lexus convertible I love to drive. I've traveled all over Europe and lived in San Francisco, Los Angeles, and Seattle. I went back to school and became a Certified Divorce Coach so

I could help others get through the divorce process because I made a lot of mistakes that I hope to help them avoid. But I do it mostly because it fulfills me; I've learned that fulfillment brings happiness.

Bottom line, I'm grateful for the life I have now and love every single day. There are so many opportunities I've had that I never dreamed could happen to me. My ex ended up living somewhere that I could never have been happy (cold and remote), and he is now remarried. I can truly say that I am happy for him and even happier for me. He did me a favor; I just couldn't see it then. **So, as you begin this process, know that the end will come, but it's really a beginning.**

While you are going through your divorce, expect to be in a bit of a fog. Things may not feel like they are really happening, or your feelings may just seem flat without a lot of enthusiasm for anything going on around you. It's okay; we all go through it, and we all come out the other side. It takes at least a year from the date your divorce is final, and I mean decree-in-hand final, to get your feet on the ground. Some say it takes half the life of the marriage to get back to yourself, but if you were in a long-term marriage, giving your ex another five to ten years is ridiculous! Just keep in mind that you don't want to make any major decisions like getting remarried or changing careers during the first year. Give yourself time to heal and get your feet on the ground.

Common Post-Divorce Issues

Remember, the first year after your divorce should be a time to heal and plan. It's not a time to make major decisions but to wrap up the loose ends from your settlement and plan what you want to do moving forward as a liberated single person. Get to know, like, and accept your new self.

You will be tired of paying legal fees, but it will be well worth the investment to have your attorney help you finish the transfer of property after the divorce decree is issued. They will help you make sure the proper paperwork is filed. They can also guide you in having the *transfer and assumptions* to get your names on the right assets and debts.

Spousal Support Modification

Sometimes life changes right when you think things will be settling down. If there is a significant change of circumstances such as losing your job or having to relocate, there are remedies that may help you financially. You may be paying spousal support and not be able to afford the payments while you are looking for a new job, or you may need more support while you are finding something new. Either way, this would normally qualify as a significant change in circumstances, and the court allows you to ask for a modification of support temporarily. The key is that it must be a significant change of circumstances, not that you just feel it wasn't fair in the initial ruling.

Relocating Out of State

If you are a parent, it can be more difficult since your move will affect your child's relationship with the other parent and relatives. The other parent's permission or court order is typically required before you can move a child out of state.

If the other parent won't agree to the move, the court will consider their relationship with your child, relationships with other relatives, and their activities and schooling. If the move is because you are getting a better job with more money that will give the child a better lifestyle or medical care, that is considered as well. The judge will take this all under advisement and rule based on what they feel is in the best interest of the child.

No matter what, **you must do things legally** and consider what is in the best interest of your child. The ramifications can be great if you don't carefully follow the law.

Unresolved Property Issues

A divorce only covers the rights between the divorced spouses, not the rights of third parties such as mortgage companies or retirement and investment accounts. You will want to make sure that these are correctly divided using the proper legal means; even though you are tired of paying your attorney, you should retain them until these loose ends are tied up.

A retirement, for example, will need a **qualified domestic relations order (QDRO),** which is a very complex document allowing the tax-free transfer of funds from one retirement account to another. This will need to be done by an accountant and possibly your HR department, but it is imperative that it is done correctly, or it could bite you later when you go to access your retirement.

You will also want to transfer any deeds that need to change hands from one of you to the other, such as car titles. Your will also needs to be changed, as the beneficiary was most likely your spouse before the divorce. They will automatically be revoked as the beneficiary upon divorce in most states, and any money or property would go to your alternate beneficiary. You will want to update your will.

You will also want to send a copy of your divorce decree to any creditors that hold a debt that was awarded to your ex. Ask what needs to happen to have your name removed from the debt and follow up on it. They will either want the debt to be refinanced or assumed by the other party. Until this happens, you are at risk of your credit being hurt should your ex skip a payment.

Finally, run a full credit report and make sure that all debts on it are either transferred or refinanced so the correct name is on it. Even if you are not worried about them making the payments, the debt-to-income ratio could affect your ability to get financing should you need it.

Remarriage

Close to 80 percent of divorced people go on to remarry within four years, though younger adults tend to remarry faster than older adults. If you are considering remarriage, you need to think about the financial ramifications as well as the effect on your children.

Often your childcare arrangements have settled into an informal agreement that works for both of you, but when one wants to remarry, the other might challenge the agreement. You should also consider that you will lose a lot of your ability to file a claim against your ex once you are remarried; however, your ex can still file for a modification against you.

If you have spousal support in your favor, this will normally end when you remarry. If you are paying spousal support, you need to consider whether you can afford to continue that support and support a new household as well. You could even end up paying more because your household income rises.

Future finances may be a concern as well. You may want to consider protecting your children's inheritance by providing a living income for your spouse but keeping the bulk of the inheritance for your children.

My Ex Won't Pay

Even though the court ordered your ex to pay child support, that doesn't mean it's going to happen. There are legal protections there for you, but first try to find out why they aren't paying and see if you can work something out. They may just need a couple of months to catch up.

If that doesn't work, the Child Support Enforcement Amendments of 1984 can help. They allow district attorneys to help you collect. They will serve your ex with papers telling them to meet with the DA's office to set up a payment arrangement and warn them that failing to follow these instructions could be met with jail time. That said, jail time is a last resort because your ex can't earn money while they are in jail, so it is counterproductive. Some of their other remedies are:

- Withholding tax refunds
- Garnishing wages
- Seizing property

- Suspending occupational and business licenses
- Revoking their driver's license

The National Child Support Enforcement Association is a good resource that will provide a list of agencies that are there to help enforce your child support orders. If your ex moves out of state, you can enforce child support through the Uniform Interstate Family Support Act. The Deadbeat Parents Punishment Act makes it a felony for a parent to refuse to pay child support to a parent living in another state.

If your ex isn't paying, you should contact the attorney that handled your custody case in the beginning if you can afford it. If you can't afford an attorney, you should contact the Department of Child Support Services in your community, and they will help you enforce, collect, or modify your child support. This government agency is there to act on behalf of the court in making sure children receive financial support. You will find your local office by going to the federal Office of Child Support Enforcement website and clicking the "Find a Child Support Agency Near You" link.

Don't panic. The government takes child support very seriously and has safety nets there to help you receive it. They always act with the best interest of the children as a priority.

CHAPTER EIGHT

Gray Divorce, Same-Sex Marriage, and Citizenship

As of 2019, divorce rates are seeing their steepest rise among two groups: same-sex couples and retirees. While these demographics share many of the issues outlined so far in this book, this chapter is dedicated to outlining special circumstances and legal challenges these groups need to consider. It also will offer advice regarding residency and documentation for US immigrants facing divorce.

Three Very Different Divorces

A recent client came to me who had been married for 32 years. She found a receipt for rent for a nearby apartment and confronted her husband. He quickly told her he wanted a divorce. He was a CPA with his own practice, and she, though college educated, hadn't worked full-time in 20 years. They had two children in their early 20s. Like a lot of boomer couples, he had always controlled the finances; he told her that if she held her temper, he would be fair with her.

Their marital assets consisted mostly of his lucrative CPA practice and their marital home, as they had put most of their money into their children and their college educations. When the CPA practice was appraised, most of the value was given to the "goodwill and personal skills" of the husband, which can't be divided easily. Living in a state that doesn't give alimony easily, the outlook for my client was bleak. She would have to go back to work, and her lifestyle would suffer immensely. They finally settled with her receiving all the equity in the home, which had to be sold. She moved to a smaller place and found a new job writing children's books, something she'd always thought about doing but never pushed herself to explore.

More than half of the divorces over 50 are marriages of less than 10 years; however, there is still a significant percentage that have been married 30 years or more. Studies show that divorce in this group greatly increases the risk of poverty. Older couples who are divorced have only 20 percent of the wealth that their married counterparts have, and divorced women over 65 have an 80 percent greater chance of being impoverished than divorced males. Add this statistic to the rate of divorce among remarried couples, and the outlook is grim.

LGBTQ+ divorces are also getting more complicated. States that didn't recognize gay marriage prior to the Supreme Court ruling in 2015 have created new legal messes to deal with. Because the laws are inconsistent, some who thought they were divorced are finding they aren't, and others are having to litigate just for legal rights to their children.

This was the situation for a lesbian couple in Mississippi. The couple, who had been together since 1999 and married since 2009 (in a state where it was legal), have been trying to get divorced and determine custody of their two boys. Two years before they could legally marry, they decided to adopt a child, but since same-sex couples couldn't marry or adopt children in Mississippi at that time, one of them adopted the six-year-old child on her own and is the only parent listed on the adoption papers. The boy lived with them both until their separation. Additionally, two years after the adoption, they used in vitro fertilization to have another child. The same partner who had adopted carried the child and could only list herself on the birth certificate by law in Mississippi.

They lived together and raised the two boys together for several years until their marriage fell apart. The divorce got ugly when the legal mother alleged the other was abusive and couldn't hold down a job. The other woman said she had worked for most of the marriage but had taken a year off to raise the boys after they had brought them home. She vehemently disagreed that she had ever been abusive.

They moved apart in 2013, but when trying to file for divorce, they were told they would have to go to the state where they had married. That state said they would have to live there for a year before they could divorce.

The mother of the boys remarried a year later thinking her marriage wasn't recognized in their state, but when the court legalized same-sex marriage two years later, their divorce and her new marriage came into question.

A judge found that they were still legally married, and the new marriage was void, so they proceeded to file for divorce and fight for custody. The mother whose name is not on the paperwork has an uphill battle, even though she can prove she was there to help raise the boys until they separated and she voluntarily sent child support to the other mother.

The legal mother at this point said her ex had no rights to the boys and alleged that she had been abusive and unreliable. She had not been allowed to see the boys for over a year and was arguing that if the children had come to them during the marriage, they would have been children of the marriage and both names should be on the birth and adoption certificates.

The case still hasn't been decided in the courts, but when it is, it will establish whether the nonlegal mother's name should be added to the younger boy's birth certificate and whether she will get custody and visitation rights.

Though this is a complicated case, it is not that unusual for LGBTQ+ couples to run into issues like this since the laws are new and no precedents have been set. These two women raised the two kids for 10 years, which shows the intention of building a family and may hold weight in the court, but the decision will be a big one for many couples. These are just a few of the complex issues to be decided in the next few years that will have a great impact on divorces for LGBTQ+ couples, since the laws are slow to catch up with the reality in which we now live.

Then there's Sonja. After years of long-distance dating, Sonja entered the country on a K3 visa and married her husband John. They soon found out, however, that they were incompatible and not meant to be married after all. Because the marriage was shorter than two years, protecting her immigration status can be complicated.

They will enter a joint submission form together proving the marriage was well intentioned. If both entered the marriage on a *bona fide* (good faith) basis, they could indicate this to the immigration authorities through submitting a jointly signed form requesting the conditional residence, and the proof of the marriage might be enough to overcome a threat of marriage fraud.

If John, however, refuses to be amicable and help her, she will need to request a waiver of the joint submission request and explain why. It will say that the ending of the marriage was not her fault or intention. Immigration is normally understanding that marriages don't always succeed and should not punish the spouse for a divorce based on irreconcilable differences that could not be solved with counseling.

If immigration has reasonable grounds to believe that this marriage was solely to obtain an immigration benefit, they will deny the request for an extended visa.

Gray Divorce

When you are in your 20s and 30s, you still have many years ahead to work and save for your future, but older people need a larger share of the household income and resources for their future. Statistics show that **a single person over 65 needs 79 percent of a two-person household income to maintain a decent lifestyle**. One needs to ask themselves at this age if they can support themselves now and, more importantly, for the rest of their lives.

It is important to look at the value of an asset today but also its potential for growth, security, and tax incentives during the property division. You want some liquid assets that can be accessed immediately if necessary but also some that will have long-term growth and payout potential. It will be a good investment to see a financial analyst so that you have a road map for your retirement. You may feel that you have enough to last the rest of your life, but this can change very quickly if you make poor financial decisions. If you've never managed money or investments, it's crucial to have a financial advisor telling you what you can spend and how to invest properly so that you have financial stability.

Social Security Benefits

You can still get Social Security if you are divorced, but there are certain rules. To qualify, you must have been married for over 10 years, both of you must be at least 62 before you can claim benefits, you must not be remarried, you must be divorced for two years or longer, or your ex must already be claiming their benefits.

Based on the preceding criteria, your benefit would be 50 percent of your ex's monthly amount, as long as you claim at your full retirement age (FRA). The amount is determined by the age you decide to start taking it. If you wait to begin receiving retirement benefits at your normal full retirement age, you will get a higher amount; however, you can claim as early as 62, but you will receive less than half the amount you would by waiting.

Your ex might do things to complicate your life, but Social Security is off-limits. They have no influence over your benefits, so when you want to start your Social Security benefit, you just take your documents that prove the marriage and divorce to an appointment with your local SSA office. They will calculate your benefits, and assuming you meet the preceding criteria, you'll start getting the higher benefit based on your ex-spouse's Social Security amount.

Retirement Accounts

When you divorce, your attorney will either hire a specialist or do the paperwork very carefully when it comes to dividing retirements. You will most likely require a court order called a qualified domestic relations order (QDRO) that covers the division of retirement benefits. Prior to any decisions on retirements, you should get a copy of the summary plan description from the retirement plan administrator for your lawyer. You will also want to talk to your lawyer about when you can receive distributions and avoid tax penalties, whether you get survivor benefits if your ex dies first, whether there are any loans taken out against a 401(k) that need to be repaid before dividing funds, if you are entitled to any contributions made after the divorce, whether you can take a hardship withdrawal if needed, and whether survivors benefits apply if you are a civilian spouse with military retirement involved.

Funds that are added to retirement accounts during a marriage are considered marital property in most states, but funds either of you started the marriage with already in a retirement account are generally considered separate property.

If your spouse has a defined contribution plan like a 401(k), the timing of your payment may depend on the specific plan. Some will make immediate lump sum payouts while others might make periodic future payments. A defined benefit plan like a company pension will likely pay you monthly payments once you hit normal retirement age.

Determining how much you will get from the division of retirement assets is very important when planning your life after the divorce. Whether you have other sources of retirement income added to the amount you receive in your divorce will help in planning a retirement budget.

Alimony

There isn't a formula for determining the amount and duration of spousal maintenance when the parties have been married over 20 years and the party seeking alimony is over 50 years old, but some states support an open-ended award of alimony if one spouse is still working and makes a disproportionate income. This is sometimes misnamed as a "lifetime award" because it is normally modifiable.

No matter what, it will end at the death of either spouse or remarriage of the receiving spouse except when the parties both agree that spousal support will be non-modifiable. This means that if there is a significant change in circumstances for either spouse, they can seek to modify or terminate the award. This often happens if there is a disability or retirement of the paying spouse.

If both spouses are retired, they might try to even out the retirement income of both parties through property settlement like a larger share of equity in the home or through a disproportionate share of the retirement in a 401(k) or other account that can be split. This allows the party with the retirement to keep it intact.

Talking to Grandchildren

Gray divorce can send shock waves throughout the family if you don't live together anymore and people are not aware of the disagreements or deterioration of the relationship on a daily basis. Not only does it affect your children, but it affects their children as well.

In an effort to maintain the grandchildren's sense of faith in marriage and security, you need to be especially careful to not put your grandchildren in the middle. Just as you would do with your children if you had divorced earlier, try not to ever speak ill of their other grandparent or place blame; it will only damage your own relationship with them.

Studies show that it is harder for a grandfather to maintain a close relationship with his grandchildren after a divorce, so take note and try to encourage this relationship. There are a few steps you can take to help your grandchildren through this time:

- Try to spend time with them as much as possible and keep it light and fun.
- Handle your relationship with your ex-spouse carefully; you will probably see them at the grandchildren's events in the future.
- Show understanding when it comes to holidays and events in the future.
- Be the calm in the storm for them, the steady rudder in a sea of change.

Domestic Partnership and Same-Sex Marriage

In 2015, the US Supreme Court recognized the right of same-sex partners to legally marry through its decision in *Obergefell v. Hodges*. The decision said that same-sex couples "have a constitutional right to marry in all states and have their marriage recognized by other states." This also meant that same-sex couples could share Social Security and other benefits afforded traditionally married couples.

James Obergefell, the plaintiff in the case, wanted his husband's Ohio death certificate to list him as the surviving spouse. He said after the case that "today's ruling from the Supreme Court affirms what millions across the country already know to be true in our hearts: that our love is equal."

He hoped that the term "gay marriage" would soon be known simply as "marriage." However, with marriage comes divorce, and the country is still evolving legally in how to approach the complex issues in same-sex divorce.

Differences between Domestic Partnerships and Same-Sex Marriages

Domestic partnerships are rare now that same-sex marriage is legal in all states because they originally came about to offer an alternative to those who couldn't legally marry. They are like marriages in that they are a state-recognized way to formalize a romantic relationship between two people who seek benefits like those given to married couples.

There are only 10 states—and Washington, DC—that recognize domestic partnerships: California, New Jersey, Colorado, Maine, Maryland, Nevada, Oregon, Washington, Hawaii, and Wisconsin.

Different parts of the United States, and even the world, recognize domestic partnerships differently, with some granting the same rights as they do traditional marriage while others draw more of a distinction between the two. Location plays a big role. In the United States, marriage rights are much more consistent than domestic partnerships.

Benefits and protections given by your state or city are the biggest differences between marriage and domestic partnerships because there is no national mandate by the federal government for those in a domestic partnership. New York City, for example, gives the same benefits to city employees in both marriages and domestic partnerships, while Washington, DC, has practically the same inheritance, alimony, and childcare laws for both. It's important to have a good attorney who knows the specific laws in your location. Some places only allow domestic partnerships if one partner is over the age of 62.

Many companies finally got to where they would offer benefits to a domestic partner just like a spouse; however, when same-sex marriage was legalized and they had to offer benefits to the spouse, they rolled back those programs and gave the couples in a domestic partnership two years to decide to get married or lose those benefits.

In most places, a domestic partnership ends the same way as a traditional marriage. You go through the whole divorce process; you can file separately if you want, and the laws of your state or city will determine the terms of your settlement. Domestic partnerships can only be terminated in the states that recognize them, and you may have to prove at least six months of residency before you file. Uniquely, California offers a termination of domestic partnership if it has lasted less than five years and there are no children involved; otherwise, it will need to go through the court process.

Property Division

Dividing assets and determining alimony can get complicated when same-sex couples divorce since they may have been together for years before they could legally marry. Determining when the marriage actually began—even if it wasn't legal—can weigh heavily into the decisions on property division and spousal support.

The courts are given a great deal of discretion in making these decisions because they can change the outcome so much. If a couple lived together for 18 years and then were legally married for two years, the court must determine if they were married for two years or two decades. If the judge decides to tack on the years of cohabitation, it can be beneficial to the lower-income-earning spouse, but if the judge goes the other route and calls it a two-year marriage, the lower-income partner may get nothing.

The same complications apply to child custody. Whether a child was born to or adopted by only one of the partners due to the laws at the time can impact the legal parental rights of the other partner. This can get very complicated and ugly in the courts if the parent with legal rights wants to stand in the way of the other parent having a relationship with the child.

Pet Custody

An intense dispute can be created over pets in divorce. Pets are usually treated as property that can be distributed in most states; however, in 2018 a new law went into effect in Illinois that treats pets more like children, and pets can now be the subject of a custody order. This is similar to laws in Alaska, where the best interest of the pet is considered when determining a fair arrangement. In California, the judge can assign sole or joint custody of the pet and even award temporary orders on the custody of the pet while the divorce process is progressing. Pet owners can also be given joint custody in the divorce order. This only applies to companion animals, however, not to service animals that would stay with the person needing them.

If you can't work out an arrangement yourselves, the court has wide discretion to work out an arrangement for you. They will consider who provides the most care of the animal by taking the pet on walks and to the vet and then award the pet to the person most involved with the pet care.

If you are considering shared-care or the judge is looking at joint custody, you should think about the distance and logistics of traveling back and forth, the comfort of sleeping in a new home, separation anxiety, and other nervous behaviors that the pet might exhibit. Finances should also be considered, like who will pay the vet bills, grooming, day care, and other expenses. Is the dog healthy and young enough to handle joint custody and the upheaval it might involve, or should they stay in one place with visits that don't include overnight stays?

Set aside emotions and put your pet's needs first. It is a difficult decision, but their quality of life needs to be your top priority.

Jurisdiction

Prior to the 2015 Supreme Court ruling that legalized same-sex marriage in all states, married couples who had moved to a state that didn't recognize their marriage would be barred from getting a divorce there. They could legally get divorced in the state where they were married, but states usually have a residency requirement before a divorce can be granted. If a couple had a destination wedding and then returned to their home state where the marriage wasn't recognized, they could have a problem should they seek a divorce. Many states don't require residency to marry, just to divorce.

California requires at least one of the spouses to live in the state for six months prior to filing for divorce; however, in recognition of the challenge facing same-sex couples, they allowed same-sex couples to dissolve their marriage even if they didn't live in the state as long as they were married in California and the state they lived in was one of those that didn't recognize same-sex marriage.

Since 2015 when the Supreme Court legalized same-sex marriage federally, couples can now divorce in any state if they meet the residency requirements.

Spousal Support

Spousal support (aka alimony) is more complicated in LGBTQ+ divorces. Many couples had been together for years, if not decades, prior to when same-sex marriage became legal. Because of this, determining the "length of the marriage" in spousal support considerations is difficult. There are multiple factors considered by the judge in making the determination. One is a highly disparate level of income and potential for income, such as when a neurosurgeon is married to a nurse's aide. The chances that they will ever have equal income and lifestyles are miniscule. But what if the nurse's aide worked to put the neurosurgeon through medical school and that is why their own career never progressed beyond that point? The length of the marriage and age also come into play, as does whether there are children involved.

The state you are divorcing in is a huge factor as well. Some states just don't like to award spousal support and feel it should be evened out in property division so that the parties can move on with their separate lives. California has "palimony," which is financial support for partners who aren't married but have been cohabitating in a romantic relationship for a long period of time.

The problem for same-sex couples will be determining the length of the marriage, but beyond that the typical formula used in your state to determine spousal support amounts in all divorces will be close to the same.

Child Custody

Terminating a marriage is complicated and painful, but the logistics that same-sex couples must deal with due to the evolving laws in this arena make it even more difficult, especially when it comes to a child custody battle.

If the child was adopted by both parents, the same custody proceedings will apply as to a heterosexual couple. However, many couples haven't completed the legal process needed to make them both legal parents. In the past, some agencies would rather adopt to a single parent than a gay couple, so often one person in the couple would be the legal adoptive parent on the certificate even though they raised the child together. Additionally, often couples chose to use a donor egg or sperm and in vitro fertilization to conceive a child, so only the mother would be on the birth certificate.

When this is done and the couple later arrives in divorce court, there is a problem when only one of the parents is a legal parent. This can be exacerbated if it isn't an amicable separation and the legal parent isn't willing to compromise for the good of the child.

When one spouse has legal claim over the child, the other parent may still have some custody rights if they can establish that they have created a bond and relationship with the child. This can include financial contributions as well as time, responsibilities, and experiences.

Because the law is still evolving, it is difficult to determine what the court will decide. That is why it is important to talk to an attorney and find out how the courts tend to rule in your county if you can't work out a custody agreement together or with a mediator.

The Pregnant Man

Thomas Beatie, born in 1974, was the first girl born to his family in Hawaii. He started to self-identify with the male gender at age 10 yet as a teenager was a model and Miss Hawaii Teen USA. When he graduated from college with his MBA, he was a black belt tournament champion in Tae Kwon Do.

Beatie had sex reassignment surgery in 2002 at 28 years old and changed his sex marker from female to male officially on his state and federal identity documents. Before getting married, he officially changed his name to Thomas using Tracy (his first name at birth) as his middle name.

In a legal heterosexual marriage, Thomas married Nancy Gillespie in Hawaii on February 5, 2003. He was listed as male on his insurance and health care policies. He and his wife moved to Oregon in 2005 and decided to start a family. However, due to a prior hysterectomy, his wife couldn't carry a child. For this reason, Beatie chose to carry a baby himself, since he still had his female reproductive organs.

After writing an article in 2008 for national LGBT magazine *The Advocate,* he was the object of intense media attention. It included a shirtless picture of Beatie while pregnant and became the object of international interest, with him being dubbed "the pregnant man."

Though attracting criticism, the media attention also sparked discussion about our ideas surrounding sex and gender. In 2008, he made his first television appearance on *The Oprah Winfrey Show,* where they discussed his right to bear a child independent of his gender and that it wasn't just a female instinct to want a family. Many media outlets soon carried the story, and the paparazzi were outside the hospital when the first baby was born.

In 2012, Nancy filed for a divorce, and the news quickly hit the media. Supervised visits three times a week were all Nancy was allowed, and in the final divorce decree, Thomas was awarded sole custody of his children and had to pay alimony to Nancy.

The judge stated that because Beatie had given birth, he was legally female and therefore the marriage was not recognized in the state of Arizona. A superior court judge then issued an order suggesting that the lower court didn't have jurisdiction over the matter. This was the first case of its kind where a legal male gave birth to a child in a traditional marriage.

Since the children were legally adopted by both parents in Oregon, Thomas was listed as the father and Nancy as the mother. After a trial, the court ruled that it had a lack of subject-matter jurisdiction to grant the Beatie's divorce, and Arizona was not forced to accept their out-of-state birth or marriage certificates. Joint custody was awarded to both parents, but Beatie no longer had to pay $240 a month in alimony since the marriage was not recognized.

In 2014, an appeals court declared that the marriage was indeed valid and they could get divorced. It also stated that Beatie shouldn't have to undergo a sterilization surgery to become legally male.

Beatie later remarried the children's caregiver, and the two now have another child who was carried by his new wife.

Divorce and Immigration

Immigrants to the United States face extra scrutiny when it comes to their marriages. US Citizenship and Immigration Services (USCIS) checks for fraudulent marriages that are for the purpose of getting US citizenship. There are many requirements to ensure that only valid marriages are entered into by US citizens when immigration benefits are being sought.

Though many people do attempt fraudulent marriages for citizenship purposes, the marriages often do not last long enough for the citizenship to come to fruition and end in divorce. The USCIS also realizes real couples with valid marriage intentions can have issues and get divorced as well, though, so there are options available to stay in the system. The policies used in determining your status depend on how long you have been in the immigration process and your ability to convince them that the marriage had the right intentions to start with.

In this section we will discuss the immigration process and offer some advice regarding immigration issues and divorce.

I-130 Visa Petition

If you filed form I-130 (initial petition for immigration) and received approval, you still don't have any immigration rights. Therefore, if a spouse filed on your behalf and you then get divorced, you will not be able to move forward in the immigration process.

Typically, a couple must remain married for an immigrant to move to the next step, which is filing an immigrant visa application (form I-485) or adjustment of status. If they are divorced in the interim, the I-130 becomes invalid, which stops any green card (visa) application attached to it. Quotas on the number of visas that can be issued often make the wait for a visa close to two years. There are exceptions such as a Battered Spouse Petition, which may allow the process to continue in the case of divorce. Otherwise, when you attend your I-485 interview, your visa application will be denied due to the divorce.

Joint Residency

The spouse of a US citizen who lives in the United States will be eligible for naturalization because of their marriage; however, they must have been continuously living in the United States after becoming a legal permanent resident for at least three years. They also must have lived in marital union with the citizen spouse for at least the preceding three years before they can file for naturalization. If the marriage is terminated prior to the applicant taking the Oath of Allegiance, they will be ineligible for US citizenship. The only exception is when one can prove abuse and battery, which has specific rules and would require an attorney to help you.

Separation Instead of Divorce

You are in a better position to get your green card the further along in the process you are when you separate. This applies to a legal separation, not necessarily living apart while you work on your relationship.

If you are already separated when you have your green card interview, the ability to move forward will depend on your state laws. In some states, a legal separation automatically turns into a divorce after a certain amount of time, so the immigration authority will consider it the same as divorce and deny your green card. Other states, though, consider separation less apt to lead to divorce and leave you a possibility to receive your green card. It would involve providing evidence that the marriage remains real and you're working on it, like a written statement from a marriage counselor you are seeing. A lawyer would be advisable to assess your own state's laws.

If you have received conditional residence (first two years) before separating, but your spouse won't agree to help you file the joint petition, you can wait until the divorce is final, file for a waiver of the joint petition, and apply for permanent residence by yourself. This requires that you prove your marriage was real to start with and can be difficult if the divorce isn't final before the petition and waiver request must be filed. A lawyer can be helpful here in getting the USCIS to delay the final decision on your request until the divorce is final.

If you have already received permanent residence status before the separation, your residency shouldn't be in danger; however, you'll have to wait five years to apply for citizenship because your married status allowing you to wait only three years will no longer apply. You may also be asked at your naturalization interview to once again prove that your marriage that allowed you entry was not a sham, even though it didn't last.

CONCLUSION

I'm sorry that you are going through a divorce. It is painful and difficult for all who experience it. That said, try to remember that half of us will go through it at least once in our lives. The way your divorce goes is half up to you: you can choose to take the high road and walk away with your head held high and a decent settlement, or you can fight every step of the way, spend a lot of money on attorneys and court, ruin any chance of a relatively civil relationship going forward . . . and still walk away with just a "decent" settlement. The only difference will be whether you choose to work out as much as possible yourselves or you choose to let the courts make the decisions about your life for you. I hope this book will give you some guidance in what to expect on the road ahead and remind you that sometimes the high road is actually the easier road. Try to look at this time as a beginning rather than an ending, and the next phase of life is the adventure you create.

FINANCIAL CHECKLIST

Spouse 1

HOUSEHOLD

Monthly mortgage or rent	$_____
Monthly property taxes (if not included in mortgage)	$_____
Monthly insurance on residence	$_____
Monthly condo maintenance fee or homeowner's association fee	$_____
Monthly electricity	$_____
Monthly water, garbage, and sewer	$_____
Monthly telephone, cell phone	$_____
Monthly fuel oil, natural gas	$_____
Monthly repairs and maintenance	$_____
Monthly lawn care	$_____
Monthly pool maintenance	$_____
Monthly pest control	$_____
Monthly misc. household	$_____
Monthly food and home supplies	$_____
Monthly meals outside home	$_____
Monthly internet/cable TV	$_____
Monthly alarm service contract	$_____

Monthly service contracts on appliances	$_____
Monthly housekeeping service	$_____
Other: _____	$_____
_____	$_____

AUTOMOBILE

Monthly gasoline and oil	$_____
Monthly repairs	$_____
Monthly auto tags	$_____
Monthly car insurance	$_____
Monthly payments (lease or financing)	$_____
Monthly tolls and parking	$_____
Other: _____	$_____

MONTHLY INSURANCE

Health insurance	$_____
Life insurance	$_____
Dental insurance	$_____
Other: _____	$_____

OTHER MONTHLY EXPENSES NOT LISTED PREVIOUSLY

Monthly dry cleaning	$_____
Monthly clothing	$_____
Monthly medical, dental, and prescription (unreimbursed only)	$_____

Monthly psychiatric, psychological, or counselor (unreimbursed only)	$_____
Monthly non-prescription medication, cosmetics, toiletries, and sundries	$_____
Monthly grooming (haircut, etc.)	$_____
Monthly gifts	$_____
Monthly pet expenses	$_____
Monthly club dues and membership	$_____
Monthly sports and hobbies	$_____
Monthly entertainment	$_____
Monthly periodicals/books/tapes/CDs	$_____
Monthly vacations	$_____
Monthly religious organizations	$_____
Monthly bank charges/credit card fees	$_____
Monthly education expenses	$_____
Other: _____	$_____

CREDIT PAYMENTS (CREDIT CARDS, OTHER LOANS)

Name of creditor(s)	Balance	Payment
_____	$_____	$_____
_____	$_____	$_____
_____	$_____	$_____
_____	$_____	$_____
_____	$_____	$_____

Spouse 2

HOUSEHOLD

Monthly mortgage or rent	$_____
Monthly property taxes (if not included in mortgage)	$_____
Monthly insurance on residence	$_____
Monthly condo maintenance fee or homeowner's association fee	$_____
Monthly electricity	$_____
Monthly water, garbage, and sewer	$_____
Monthly telephone, cell phone	$_____
Monthly fuel oil, natural gas	$_____
Monthly repairs and maintenance	$_____
Monthly lawn care	$_____
Monthly pool maintenance	$_____
Monthly pest control	$_____
Monthly misc. household	$_____
Monthly food and home supplies	$_____
Monthly meals outside home	$_____
Monthly internet/cable TV	$_____
Monthly alarm service contract	$_____
Monthly service contracts on appliances	$_____
Monthly housekeeping service	$_____
Other: _____	$_____
_____	$_____

AUTOMOBILE

Monthly gasoline and oil	$_____
Monthly repairs	$_____
Monthly auto tags	$_____
Monthly car insurance	$_____
Monthly payments (lease or financing)	$_____
Monthly tolls and parking	$_____
Other: _____	$_____

MONTHLY INSURANCE

Health insurance	$_____
Life insurance	$_____
Dental insurance	$_____
Other: _____	$_____

OTHER MONTHLY EXPENSES NOT LISTED PREVIOUSLY

Monthly dry cleaning	$_____
Monthly clothing	$_____
Monthly medical, dental, and prescription (unreimbursed only)	$_____
Monthly psychiatric, psychological, or counselor (unreimbursed only)	$_____
Monthly non-prescription medication, cosmetics, toiletries, and sundries	$_____
Monthly grooming (haircut, etc.)	$_____
Monthly gifts	$_____

Monthly pet expenses	$_____
Monthly club dues and membership	$_____
Monthly sports and hobbies	$_____
Monthly entertainment	$_____
Monthly periodicals/books/tapes/CDs	$_____
Monthly vacations	$_____
Monthly religious organizations	$_____
Monthly bank charges/credit card fees	$_____
Monthly education expenses	$_____
Other: _____	$_____

CREDIT PAYMENTS (CREDIT CARDS, OTHER LOANS)

Name of creditor(s)	Balance	Payment
_____	$_____	$_____
_____	$_____	$_____
_____	$_____	$_____
_____	$_____	$_____
_____	$_____	$_____

RESOURCES

Books

Boole, Whitney. *You Got This: Healing through Divorce.* Self-published by Whitney Boole, 2019.

Doak, Debra. *High-Conflict Divorce for Women.* Berkeley, CA: Rockridge Press, 2019.

Doskow, Emily. *Nolo's Essential Guide to Divorce*, 7th ed. Nolo, 2018.

Dukhan, Helen M. *Nothing Says a Good Day Like a Divorce . . . If You Prepare for It!* Self-published by Helen M. Dukhan, 2019.

Kirshenbaum, Mira. *Too Good to Leave, Too Bad to Stay: A Step-by-Step Guide to Help You Decide Whether to Stay In or Get Out of Your Relationship.* New York: Plume, 1997.

Kübler-Ross, Elisabeth. *On Death and Dying.* New York: Scribner, 2014.

Landers, Jeffrey. *Divorce: Think Financially, Not Emotionally*, 2nd ed. San Clemente, CA: Sourced Media Books, 2015.

Maker, Azmaira H., and Polona Lovsin. *Family Changes: Explaining Divorce to Children.* San Diego, CA: Aspiring Families Press, 2015.

McBride, Jean. *Talking to Children about Divorce: A Parent's Guide to Healthy Communication at Each Stage of Divorce*. Berkeley, CA: Althea Press, 2016.

Priebe, Heidi. *This Is Me Letting You Go*. CreateSpace Independent Publishing, 2016.

Sember, Brette. *The Complete Divorce Organizer & Planner*. Self-published by Sember Resources, 2017.

Trafford, Abigail. *Crazy Time: Surviving Divorce and Building a New Life*, 3rd ed. New York: William Morrow Paperbacks, 2014.

Websites

Divorcemag.com

Divorcenet.com

Divorcesource.com

Rocketlawyer.com

REFERENCES

Florida Courts. *Final Judgment of Dissolution of Marriage with Dependent or Minor Child(ren)*. Accessed March 21, 2020. flcourts.org/content/download/403349 /3458428/990c1.pdf.

Hgoldstein.com. *Massachusetts Rules of Domestic Relations Procedure—Supplement Rule 410*. Accessed March 21, 2020. hgoldstein.com/forms/rule410.htm.

Jacobs Berger, LLC. *Understanding Your NJ Divorce Settlement Agreement*. Accessed March 15, 2020. jacobsberger .com/understanding-your-divorce-settlement-agreement.

Kevin Hickey Law Partners. *How Much Will My Divorce Cost?* Accessed March 18, 2020. kevinhickeylaw.com /legal-blog/how-much-will-my-divorce-cost.

Orange County Divorce Court. *Marital Settlement Agreements and Stipulated Judgments in California*. Accessed March 21, 2020. orangecountydivorce.com/marital-settlement -agreements-stipulated-judgments.

Rembert, Elizabeth. "Letter from the Editor: The Stigma around Divorce Needs to Change." *Daily Nebraskan*. November 16, 2018. dailynebraskan.com/opinion/letter-from-the-editor -the-stigma-around-divorce-needs-to/article_0f0ee85e -e94a-11e8-b974-97389e92b700.html.

INDEX

ACKNOWLEDGMENTS

I would like to thank my children, Jessica, Logan, and Claire . . . and my ex, Mike. Without all of you, I wouldn't be the person I am today. That said, if I could go back and change how our divorce went, I would. Thankfully, a bad divorce doesn't negate the good times we had as a family and the memories we all hold dear.

I'm grateful that we have all learned to focus on the good times and let go of the bad. In other words, we've learned to forgive. I've always believed it's during the hardest times that your soul grows the most, but no parent wants to see their children hurt, and there's no way around it: divorce hurts.

I'd also like to thank Tim Durkop, who started as an attorney and became a friend. His help in getting through my divorce was immeasurable. I'll always be grateful for his encouragement and confidence that I would not only survive but thrive.

Divorce is an ending and a beginning and will change parts of you forever. If you choose to accept those changes with grace and dignity, it has the power to shape your whole paradigm as you move forward to the next adventure in life. Your attitude is a choice.

If this book makes divorce just a little less painful for one person or family, then perhaps something was gained from our own divorce experience.

Thank you to my girlfriends in Coeur d'Alene, Idaho, and the Bay Area who believed in me when I sometimes didn't. Your encouragement helped me discover so many new parts of myself that I didn't even know were there. Oh, what an adventure this chapter of life has been. I wouldn't have missed it for the world!

ABOUT THE AUTHOR

 **René Vercoe**, Certified Divorce Coach, writes not only from the heart but from her own divorce experiences and those of the clients she's worked with in her coaching practice. After a 27-year marriage, she survived a brutal divorce that left her and her family deeply wounded, both emotionally and financially. On a journey to heal her own wounds, she went back to school and became a Certified Divorce Coach, determined to help others weather the storm with less pain, injury, and lasting scars.

Helping other marriages fail successfully may seem like an odd career, but healing her own wounds through helping others has been one of the best experiences of her life. In her coaching practice, she seeks to help people not only through the divorce process but also to discover themselves and their potential along the way. Instead of seeing divorce as an end, they learn to see it as the end of a phase of life and a new beginning, as well. When things seem out of control, the one thing they can control is their attitude. They can learn to look forward to the next phase of life as a new beginning full of adventure, anticipation, and confidence.

NOTES